Capitalism is a Death Cult

a poetry anthology

Sunday Mornings at the River

Capitalism is a Death Cult
©Sunday Mornings at the River, 2025

All Rights Reserved.

Sunday Mornings at the River supports copyright as we believe this fuels creativity and promotes free speech.

Thank you for complying with the copyright laws by not reproducing, scanning, or distributing any part of it in any form without permission, except for the purpose of review and promotion of the work.

Compiled, designed and edited by Rebecca Rijsdijk
rebeccarijsdijk.com for
Sunday Mornings at the River
sundaymorningsattheriver.com
@sundaymorningsattheriver

The publisher does not have any control over and does not assume any responsibility for author or third party websites and their content.

Thanks for reading.

For the ones they tried to grind down—

the care workers, the artists, the mothers,
the ones with too many jobs and not enough rest,
the ones who said no when silence was expected,
the ones who refused to become machines.

For the fallen and the furious.
For the ones still here.

This anthology is for you.

"It is no measure of health to be well adjusted to a profoundly sick society."

— Jiddu Krishnamurti

Contents

Foreword 11
Capitalism is a Death Cult 13
The Fountain of Youth...15
Acts of Rebellion 16
Rage..17
Eggshell Blues 19
God Bless This American Nightmare....................................20
Living Wage...21
The Late-Stage Capitalism Complex.....................................22
Armed, Green and Dangerous 24
A Fish in Time...25
Undefined Capitol..26
Capitalistic Donut Cycle..27
Mango Trees Slanting..29
Father Worked 31
Shame...32
Mediocrity 34
Kiel's..36
Big Bets..38
Civil 39
Dome of the Capital 41
No hay Frontera...42
We All Could Have Houses...43
Incantation: reclaim these streets..44
Why are Capitalists idolised..47

Assimilation	48
Microbots	49
Never Never	50
The Dark Tower in Fetter Lane	51
Sweet Nothings to a Neighbourhood	52
The Marketplace	53
Arithmetical Anathema	54
Dreams of the universe	55
Wilshire Blvd	56
Sandwich Board, Soapbox & Bell	57
A Hymn for the Faithful	59
The Amaltaas is in Bloom	61
20% off headstones all weekend!	63
(death to) celebrity worship	65
Can I Please have the Floor?	66
O'Brien	67
Bite the Rich	68
Job Hunting	69
Uncommitted	71
They Were Once Real	78
Auschwitz by the Sea	79
Umbrella Men	80
Necro Scene	82
Prayer for Giving Up Shopping on Amazon	83
The Cabin	85
The Borders	86
I Hear the Birds Screech Like Loose Hinges	87
The Children's United of Nation	89
Territorial	92

Crane Ballet 93
A Visit to the Dentist 94
Corporations Don't Need Passports 95
White Mail 97
From Some Hell 100
And Then You Think 102
The Midnight Zone 104
The Anatomy of Capitalism 106
The Illusion 113
To Be Pawns 114
On Ambition 119
LinkedIn 120
Humankind 121
One Week's Notice 122
Sleeping Beauties at the Met 123
Pompeii and Taxes 124
Without Compassion a Eulogy is Just Reimbursement 125
The Grocery Shopping Cult 126
The Human Cost 127
Seed-spitters 130
When the Insomniacs 131
Uncomfortable Dichotomies 132
I Don't Actually Want the Products 133
Everyone I Went to High School With Is a Realtor Now ... 135
Corrupt... 136
Solidarity 137
Neither True nor False 138
We Aren't Ready to Pay the Full Price 139
Cruel Optimism 141

The Wood-Runner's Sons 142
There Is No Money 144
Slaves to Capitalism 147
Contributors 150
About the Publisher 159

What Survives the Fire

They told us we were free.

They told us if we worked hard enough, bled quietly enough, smiled through the burn of it, we would get to the other side. The other side of what, they never said. Maybe they didn't know. Maybe they never made it there either.

I have watched the strongest people I know crumble under fluorescent lights, folding uniforms, burnt-out retinas scanning the barcode of their own exhaustion. I've held the hand of the elderly as they whispered regrets in between TV commercials and morphine drips. I've seen beauty destroyed in the name of convenience, rivers straightened, wildflowers flattened under the wheels of ambition. I have seen too much. We all have.

Capitalism is not a system—it's a theology. A death cult disguised in glossy ads and spreadsheets, preaching salvation through ownership, promising transcendence through brand loyalty. You do not leave it. You only survive it, or you don't. It colonizes not only land, but language, love, time. We are no longer people—we are consumers. No longer citizens—just data points. We are living in a machine that eats our future and sells it back to us in small, poisoned pieces.

And yet, here you are. Holding this book. Reading these words. Maybe crying. Maybe raging. Maybe both. You are not alone.

This anthology is not just a collection of poems. It's a field recording of our resistance. Each page is a smuggled seed, hidden under the tongue of someone who refused to forget how to feel. These poems are chants, dirges, battle cries, lullabies for the disillusioned, and spells for the exhausted. They are offerings to the ones who couldn't make it, and weapons for those still fighting.

This book is not hopeful in the capitalist sense. It won't tell you to manifest your dream job or romanticise your burnout. It does not believe in silver linings stapled to clouds of smoke. But it does believe in you.

It believes in rage as a sacred force. In tenderness as resistance. In mourning as a political act.

And it believes that somewhere—under the rubble, beneath the pipelines, past the algorithms and hedge funds—there is still something worth saving.

Something wild. Something ancient. Something that was never theirs to begin with.

Let's begin.

Rebecca Rijsdijk, *Bosslady Sunday Mornings at the River*
March, 2025

Capitalism is a Death Cult

by REBECCA RIJSDIJK

They call it progress,
a prayer mumbled over blistered tongues,
a hymn of machinery gnashing teeth on bone,
and the world is set ablaze to warm
the hands of the few.

In the glass temples of profit,
we kneel,
palms outstretched to the gods of scarcity,
chanting the psalms of productivity.

We are fed on numbers,
on promises that rot before the swallow,
and we call this survival—
the endless devouring of ourselves.
The invisible hand is a fist.
It strikes with the weight of centuries,
turns rivers to veins of poison,
turns soil to dust.
It builds altars from the ribs of the living,
erects monuments from the ruins of hunger.

Each skyscraper a tombstone,
each factory a mass grave.
This is no economy;
this is war in the guise of exchange,
a butcher's block for the soul.
And still, the choir sings:
buy, sell, bleed,
buy, sell, bleed,
as if the echo of it
could drown out the sound of the earth breaking.

CAPITALISM IS A DEATH CULT

But nothing lasts.
Not even the empire of greed.
The temples will crack,
their marble will grind into dust,
and the air will fill with the silence of forgotten debts.
The earth will not mourn.
It will rise.
And in its rising, it will swallow
every last lie.

The Fountain of Youth

by ALLEN ASHLEY

This drought has meant that all the rich gits
no longer get their daily fix.
They're out in the streets, flaking to bits,
in this bone-dry eco-apocalypse.

Acts of Rebellion

by SAMUEL FORBES

the economy of my body grinds to a halt.
no heart-thrum, no hammer,
no snap of tendon nor crack of muscle —

ten thousand shifting tides of salt fall still.

and somewhere, the great machine rolls on.
its pistons revolve,
shrinking air until it is impossibly small,
each detonation a cosmos born and destroyed.

not here.

here, the hot star works patiently
on our frost-capped planet.

a slow thaw,
a silent unwrapping,
the first bloom and final bead of white breath —

it's a gift. it's all a gift.

I am at peace
with this slack-jawed existence.

Rage

by CHLOE HANKS

In a selfish attempt to find solitude
from the footage of women grieving
over tiny charcoal bodies,

I come across a digital archiving
of Stevie Nicks cursing her former lover
to an eternalised haunting.

I cannot help but wonder if:
in our 3.95 billion— and shared conceptual feminine—
we felt the epitome of our rage

in the same moment,
might we survive the planet long enough
to articulate the boom?

Words, should they still exist,
might settle together as the dust once did
to liken the choking of the human race
to that of Augustus,

throats sticky with the remnants of fig.
What is poison, really, if not this?

The accumulation of women grasping
fingers around whatever they can find
in their kitchen that might earn them
a moment of free-thinking.

If not the crumbling of charred bodies
the men breathed in a war on heresy;
if not the blood from the severed heads of queens;

miasma emitted
from our dangling ragdoll bodies.

It rages down a bloodline
before settling upon the lady Diana
in the form of a poisoned dress;

and the entire planet swallows it.
Freedom beyond the jurisdiction of anger
held in dormancy.

The archive becomes echo chamber
for poetry in distillation.

I don't know what to tell you—
it festers in the belly of an ecosystem,
we succumb, or we expel—

you did this to yourself.

Eggshell Blues

by ELLEN HARROLD

Oh, fuck! The thorns have split their acres.
Championship trespassing caught on camera
though somewhat buoyed by the drag
force wrought
from splitting temperatures, bark layers exposed
by half-hearted permafrost. Take the sequetoers
to the ragged edges, or someone else will
take the hedge trimmers. Hacking away
as a cold sun pierces the din and twigs,
so delicately spun, are unravelled.
Thrown roadside
and crushed for aesthetic appeal.

God Bless This American Nightmare

by DOMINIQUE RISPOLI

the sun is out / for the first time / in a day or two / the week / dragged it's feet so slowly / that a month / felt like a year / and a week / has felt like four / when the kids have started / to lose their homes / lose their fathers / lose their identities / to this god of greed / this curse of / the political superpower / which translates to / a country built / on the backs / of those they step on / this land that they stole / and bastardized / for their own sick glory

and I am slowly / losing my sanity / living amongst / this casual carnage / so I scroll on my phone / hoping for a reprieve /but I am only met with / a sponsored video / for cute winter boots / a tantalizing nightgown / to please your man / a cat video / a lost puppy / a comedic podcast / a worried teacher / a lesbian couple / a grieving holocaust survivor / an episode of the handmaid's tale / noticing the patterns / yet I continue to scroll / to numb the dull ache / burrowing inside of my chest / protection spells / apocalyptic fires / dollar tree hauls / how to resist / where to organize / because they are watching / they are always watching / with their fists clenched / yet still I scroll / upon advice / on how to get a passport / how to get out quick/ how to stay and fight / until you can't anymore / but watch in horror / as our already precarious freedoms / slip through the cracks / of this American nightmare

Living Wage

by JOSEPH NUTMAN

Tender feet from 9 hours of £9.90 per hour,
tarsal deep ache from a shift stood
on blunt knives,
pavement cares little for your plight
– stone faced,
at the factory gates a bully of a sky awaits,
fades from baby blue to haematoma in the clouds
more a scuffle than a sunset fights
above the town.
Chill autumnal air plays the fall guy –
takes the convenient blame for the watering
of the eyes,
but I recognise you –
a fellow punch bag walking home,
your work days are fingers
imprinting on your life,
nails break the skin in all the places you can't hide.

The Late-Stage Capitalism Complex (or The Nourishment of the Climate Crisis)

by SOPH KAY

I
Excess and oblivion are
houses in the same
street /

Their lights
simultaneously luminous
and on the precipice of power outage /

II
Despair becomes a
place you can room in /

Build visions of
unattainable, sustainable
futures /

Where an absence of
liminality or nihility
is what permeates
days /

III
The all-knowing
is a profound silence.

It perforates eardrums;

The certainty
of self-inflicted
implosion
precludes prosperity /

IV
How do you
rent a house that
is owned /

by that which will be
the cause of
the end of the world?

V
When will we choose
wealth over profit? /

Armed, Green and Dangerous

by RAJANI RADHAKRISHNAN

Who will do the arithmetic of war?
Up the supply chain,
down row (after row) of bodies,
up and down the broken earth,
the fucked-up climate?
Along the line of trucks?
Around arms: loaded, dropped...maimed?

I sort needs like waste, in coloured bins.
Things I don't need.
Things that I can take back to the earth.
Things that break. Themselves. Them. Me.
Things that will grow into trees. Wants.

At the convenience store,
the young man is ringing up my needs. Uncaring.
I fill my green canvas tote. Smug.
I pretend my world is stitched whole.
I pretend I am free.

In the Uber, the news crackles.
It calls destruction, investment.
It calls death, market.
It calls profit, peace.
It calls a person, target.
It calls wants, needs.
It calls my complicity, grief.
It calls my grief, rebellion.

A plastic bag escapes from a landfill,
flutters like a white flag.

A Fish in Time

by RAJANI RADHAKRISHNAN

because the wise person said if you
give a man a fish, it may feed him for
a day, teach him how to fish instead

and the fisherman caught more than
he could ever eat and sold to the
village and sold to the town and one

thing led to another the way we know
it does until there was nothing left
in the river and nothing left in the sea

except one giant whale with a fire in its
belly and the universe said, and only
out of a fleeting pity, that it had learnt

from earth's apex predators that it
could give the whale a body to eat
that day or it could teach it to hunt

and somehow it all came full circle
and they say on a clear day you can
still see a giant fin pass in the distance.

Undefined Capitol

by SARAH BECK MATHER

competition combines death pigs
echo pigs
with inexplicable indifference
when I was little
I wandered through trees
as these
were home
now destruction to ourselves
is productive
emotional tumours
cause coldness
and hesitantly
forces growth of branches
beyond compulsion
beyond consequences
a proliferation of
air
bubbled
seeds and
cancerous
self

Capitalistic Donut Cycle

by UZOMAH UGWU

Same routine every morning
Shower, makeup, a set of clothes
laid out across the bed
A breakfast not fit for champions
but it keeps the hunger out

Car keys and a new coat
with a worn-out look from the
Sale rack on a salary cap or
would have gotten a hat

Desk, computer, co workers
and the boss all in a roll
Or better yet a perfect packaged
superficial gift that leaves most of us
At economic and social differences
while working for the same quarterly goals

Just the everyday happenings
ending in the same conclusion
With the same start
On your mark set go in perfect circles
rounding out your dreams to be pushed out

Bored and in need of support
When quitting wasn't an option to choose

So constant loss is what is written
across the mirror each time it is visited
In a shallow bathroom where life

walked back and forth
Exchanging covers of the layers
of the many faces
Stretched daily to accept a pace
that does not equate
To anything meaningful or different
Leaving questions like could this be all
And at what point does one not care if it is a loss

Mango Trees Slanting

by UZOMAH UGWU

Tall mango trees sidings
Line up walls meant not for climbing
Even though the ceiling
Must come down

Passed over hourly not just annually
All that matters most is who can
Boast the most masculinity

Depleted and tattered out
A plunger will not do to unclog
This mess at the bottom of soles
Of worked out shoes
That pace corporate floors
Trying to keep up with capitalism's rat race
Deciding on a better maneuver
To bull over this market and aim
High enough to hit the target
Seems lost in the broken glass of
name plaques outside office doors
That only include his pronouns not hers
The only equality that suits her is in the bathroom

just the opposite resides and sits at
conference room tables where they
are not even fables just visual lies
where women do not get to sit as equals
but are pushed to quit
she looks on at a workforce pit
where she is not told she is not

CAPITALISM IS A DEATH CULT

physical or mental fit just given mind games and
office politics and
given a loud pink slip or she keeps
working three jobs but only gets paid
like she is doing one
if only she were a man
this cycle would have never begun
she crossed her legs like nothing was
between her ears
as thought by her male peers
never considered a fit
because she carried tampons in her purse
it was hard for her to sit even
with RGB on the bench

Father Worked

by UZOMAH UGWU

Father worked his hands
Made it hard for him to hold his kin

All he saw was his trade
Forgot what kept his back up

Never kissed my mother anymore
While she waited inside the door for him to come home

Our house walked with his shadows
Felt the painful steps his boots knew well

Father never knew what made
Us smile or how it was once him

He worked for his death
But left nothing for his grave

So that we could live out our dreams
And outlive his

Shame

by TATE CHIMHANDA

Think back to your childhood.
That moment you were caught
with your hand deep in the cookie jar,
crumbs on your face.
Guilty as you are you feign innocence.

"It wasn't me"

How many times have you been caught out,
only to return to yearly learned patterns?
Swipe swipe swipe, until you numb.
Freedom… do we gain it upon our expiration
promotion to that higher plane?

I fear for the afterlife.
For there is a high chance it already is tainted
by the capitalist scourge…
I mean aren't the founders and pioneers
already there?
Who is to know
if they haven't already drawn borders,
partitioned that which we thought indivisible.

I came into this world with nothing
and will leave with nothing.
I correct myself.
I came into this world from love
and will leave it full of love.

The adage is.
'In Africa, it takes a village to raise a child'

Sunday Mornings at the River

Yeah, that's because the Capitalists
took all our resources.

The west and the east continue to in some way.
Investment they say, build up infrastructure.
Minerals intellect, one directional conveyor
that never stopped.
Build your dreams in a new land.

They act like they don't want us,
But need us.
Who still remain the backbone to their economies.

Hidden unappreciated, yeah send 'em back!
Free flights to the motherland even if it ain't your land.

In the West they say,
"In Africa it takes a village to raise a child".
Little do they know those villages lie shrunken.
The youth dem fled enticed by the dream
of cream on foreign shores.

Mediocrity

by NATHANIEL KRENKEL

Purple trash bags up
And down the block
A diaper, or meat

The seagull cares
Has started the day's work
Retrieving something special

For her family
Her seagull boyfriend, or maybe
A wee treat for herself

I sit down with coffee and water
To continue revising the book
About middle age, capitalism and mediocrity

But all I can think about
Is the man on the radio
Calling in to answer the morning questions

When asked
This classic sitcom about FM disc jockeys
He replied confidently, WKRP in Pittsburgh

All I can picture
Is the man on Congress Street
With half-smoked cigarettes in his ears

Sunday Mornings at the River

What does he know that I don't
I quit smoking a decade ago
And have still never been to Pittsburgh

I have so many fake names and
Half-baked fancies
It's like I was born to watch

In sum, be thankful be
Inspired by flesh and wax
Be the old's embrace of techno

Kiel's

by NATHANIEL KRENKEL

In the mid-90s
I lived on 13th Street
Between 1st and 2nd Avenues
Allen Ginsberg ate noodles
In steamy glass Mei
And Kathy showed me her thong
And down the street was Kiel's
Madonna shopped there, we heard
And I made 19K a year
But a Spotify penny I did spend
On lotions and potions
It was better than Spy
Better than the guest list
For Nancy Boy
Keil's felt cool
Like Ad Busters and No Logo
And knowing the weed delivery guy's first name
Flash Forward:
30 years, MAGA
Burning the world to own the libs
King tides and crooked cracked bridges
Adult diapers on every page
And my favourite hair item, SILK
GROOM, has been unavailable since
Pre-pandemic, so I call, down the coast
Maine to Manhattan
I beg, please, let me return to those days

Sunday Mornings at the River

When my hair was shiny and expensive
Hair weeper, that is me
The self recoiled, but progress did happen
A box arrived, Silk Groom. Now, my life
Is restored. Belief returned.
We are animals living on a planet
With other animals
TRUE OR FALSE

Big Bets

by RACHEL BERRYMAN

the world's largest Venture Capital firm has
$42 billion in assets under management

a
loss is not a loss until its
realized. until then, it's
potential. it's rounds. it's investment being
corralled and coerced into
returns. it's Angels sprinkling their
dust, I mean their
magic. risk isn't risk unless it's
downside. the Expected Value of 1 billion
times 1% likelihood of success
times 50% chance of Doom is
higher than the Expected Value
of a sustainable business model
with 0% chance of Doom, that's just
rational. we're looking for ideas that
disrupt—only then do we stand a chance
of causing realchange,
of using innovation to fix what's broken, of
guiding the invisible hand to mend a
world on the frit-
z

Civil

by FLAVIAN MARK LUPINETTI

My brother Greg
the prosecuting attorney
advises me to chill
He says the arc of the moral universe
bends toward justice
I ask did it bend toward justice
for the guy who said that
but he hasn't a clue who I mean
my clue he harvested those words
from a bumper sticker
his rosy perspective hogtied
into irrelevance by cobwebs
of complacency constructed
half a century ago

Greg hasn't attended the gun shows
boasting armouries
sufficient for overthrowing
a third world country
or a first world one
He hasn't heard
the fact-free propaganda blathered forth
by pseudo journalists
accountable only to corporate profits
I would have thought he had some familiarity
with the tsunami of corporate crime
Maybe not
Maybe that would explain his inability to see
how close this empire is coming to collapse

Why when we contemplate a future civil war
do we imagine only a rebellion of the right

yahoos in red baseball caps
rugby shirts and khaki pants
billionaire-financed police force-equipped
kidnapping a governor
or dynamiting a courthouse
What if they simply seize the levers
of government
Elections mutate into zombie referendums
All results not preordained overturned

What if we face the choice of acquiescence
or rebellion
Do we fall to fascism or select secession with
Sacramento or Boston as our latter-day Richmond

What if this time
the first person to fire
on Fort Sumter
has to be one of us

Dome of the Capital

by DANA AYMAN

Inside the dome of green,
The temple of greed,
People gather and prostrate
To a rectangular god.

Those brave enough to step forth,
offer their dearest assets,
And in turn, it offers Commodity.
For it, the elite are sacrificed.
They are bled dry then tossed away.

Its servants, dressed in gold,
feeding it human meat
and offering the gatherers gasoline.

The people sip with horror,
but there's nothing to do;
They are hungry.
And if they behave well,
they might even get to feed their god.

Outside the dome and under the merciless rain,
people are scattered on the ground,
Thin and starved holding colourful brochures
praising their rectangular god.

A slovenly man brings the lighter
close to his face,
Lights up the brochure under the rain,
and throws it into the temple out of rage.

No hay Frontera

by TOMÁS LAORNI MANOPULO

There is no border
la historia of the *mestizx* tells it.
Las fronteras are venom,
living in us all
the diaspora first.

There's no line between us,
no hay raya q nos separe
hasta when you draw
it with your thousands of
black BIC ballpoint pens,
un camello of today's slavery.

Tu border,
is really your swallowing
of *the veneno en tus pulmones*
which capitalism had you
breath since birth
like every *chinx quién*
is stepped on by *el gringo*
blanco de guanábana picha.

Footnotes:
la historia of the mestizo – the story/history of the
mixed-race person. *Las fronteras* – The borders
no hay raya q nos separe – there is no line that separates us.
veneno en tus pulmones – poison in your lungs.
Camello – a difficult job or something you have to work,
hard to produce. *chinx* – gender neutral version of china/
chino meaning child. *guanábana picha* – rotten soursop.

We All Could Have Houses

by ROBIN CHADWELL

When the mayor sets fire to our tents in winter
we tenants may choose to burn.
Must we earn our breath, too?
The blood in our veins—
blue or red—
the truth is we all could have houses
but instead, are marched naked into the woods
with that thing that we know
even when they have us on our knees:
we are born with warm skin.

Incantation: reclaim these streets

Blockupy 2013/ Hamburg 2017/ Hambi 2018/Lützerath 2023

by KATE MACALISTER

"Acts of violence against property or persons

are committed from a crowd in a manner

that endangers public safety" We change
the order, again. They call it street theatre,

('no more/mere words') [no justice, no peace] it was a
                              kind of 'music'

reclaim these streets

1. Assess the scene for safety. Do not take unnecessary risks,

you catch my gaze, link arms, I see you already dead. I saw
you broken, I saw you rise please tell me
what democracy looks like, tell me what can save us from this
economy, from always living on the edge   of
extinction, sliding beneath the starving line. Today   we
vote for the streets. all assemble, one last generation   asking
for it too politely. come and take up space with me in these
broken spaces? Mouthfuls of an unkept promise bleed upon
concrete. there are no more new worlds left   in my
stinging throat, my voice box a tired coffin ready to be
lowered. but you call to us:

reclaim, reclaim these streets

2. Stop the spread of the irritant. Get it off skin and out of the patient's eyes. Don't make it worse

remember I am the land within the wreckage, where the
fight runs like our time and you are the crashing
bathwater. ram shackled memory washed upon my hands
I hold you. remind you the only date in permanent crisis
is now. I ask you to remember these days. when we
bandage a thousand street wounds, take into our arm the
breaking world, remember the tears. the air fragrant with
the stench of blue light and gaslit fury,
remember the sound, the songs of dark times, did we ask
for this? to end up unconscripted in the war, only fought
once in a while on the concrete swarming with state
violence armed to its rotting teeth. Are we scared? No.
[whose streets?] We are put together.
like bottles. (for Molotov cocktails) are we free? safe? I
don't -
No. remember to

3. Move to a safe location.

run. breakthrough, reclaim these streets, gently - feline
    [all cats are beautiful]. sit down. take my hands,
my arms, wrap your legs around me like you loved me
once before dawn. eye to eye in each other's fire. fluidly
bonded by the spitting hisses and the call to abolish.
abolish it all. reclaim these streets. with these beaten
bodies. sink into me, mask up. there shall be rain; baton
to bone.

4. Decontaminate eyes first - flush eyes for 15 minutes

weigh into me and reclaim these streets. they fall on us
like thunder, the thudding sound of splintering, the
burning in our lungs, the clavicle pearl white in the

bloodpool below, how clear I see you now, my sister. [we are unstoppable]. cut flowers blossoming [another world is possible]

& until pain has resolved.

gathered, how we stand for hours, caught up in these cracks. is this dying or healing? and I finally feel it: this system no longer operates within this body. it is written all over our skin, my tongue.
this is a revolutionary cell signalling the end of these heavy days. how there is always another voice calling, the sound of tomorrow scratching the misty air. choking, screaming we named the monsters and called them to us. and we

5. If the pain does not resolve to a tolerable level in 45 minutes seek advanced care

reclaim these streets. we are raw and unbowed.
we are not here to play with fire we have come to burn.

Why are Capitalists idolised

By CHLOE LAWS

Someone gave you a box to live in
Then they gave you a bigger box
And called it freedom
And you lapped it up
Forgetting you don't have to live in
Those four walls

Assimilation

by AFON GOLD

I think about moving   away   on   through
don't need the   buzz   of the city
can't live the   whiteness   of the country

the outgoing home secretary   herself a her;
herself brown   says   'multiculturalism has failed'
to me; born   thinking & feeling
to a colonial   aggressor
multiculturalism
is the only   moral & righteous
outcome to our   devastation
of the lives & lineages
of all these beautiful people
here   now

I think about   the politics of Nazism

I am the enemy it imagined
their obsession   whiteness in peril
& I want it to be   I am the race traitor
in my most radical moments   thinking I would
support the banning of   white people
from mating with other   white people
because how can   whiteness
be rebranded now   dirty & cruel
as it is?

I laugh & cry   realising my solution   here
in my most   radical   pathetic
moments
is the very worst   demand
of 21st century Britain: assimilation

Microbots

By MICHAEL BRIGDEN

We are just microbots
whizzing around,
feeding the machine
that is greedily bound
to serve to a system
that is hell bent on cash
as we faithfully feed it
whilst we are knee deep in ash
of the fallen, downtrodden,
the waifs and the strays
who fell by the wayside
because they just could not pay
or help fund the system
that controls us all
so they are burnt to a cinder
and around us they fall,
we trudge through the ashes
without thought, without heed,
as long as we're happy
that we can still feed
this gargantuan machine
that relentlessly turns
and if we cannot stay focused
I am sure we will burn,
so we pretend that our choices
are for more, not for less
and that capitalism offers
all of us success.

Never Never

by EDWARD ALPORT

You know the man. He say to me,
Hey, come to me, I feel your pain,
I know the griping and the shame.
Come, let me hide me in my cloak
and let its folds enfold you,
let its shadows shade you,
and I will give you
everything you need

He say to me I never made
a promise yet I couldn't keep.
See, my hands are open. My breath is sweet.
I never lie to you,
I never trick you
to slide further into shade.
All I have is a welcoming cloak. I welcome
all of you who need.

The Dark Tower in Fetter Lane

by EDWARD ALPORT

The City wraps itself in its claggy blanket of fog,
Hunching itself around her shoulders, pulsing as I pass.
Not thick enough to hide her traps and fissures
Just to soften the edges, lie about their depth.

Brokers stride by, long legged and disdainful
Wrapping their phones in their ears, mumbling to the fog,
Long faces grimacing at the bad news, bad news
Always bad, it seems. Never seen 'em smile.

Down in a doorway, a beggar hawks a gob
And wheedles Please sir, fifty p for a cuppa.
Fifty p? Has he bought one recently?
His skinny, droop eared dog sleeps on, unconcerned.

Perhaps he knows the way, I thought, though why
I trusted him more than the brokers, sneering at my back.
I slipped him a brass one, not that it buys much tea,
But he did know the road. Down there, down there, left
there.

No traffic, in the pulsating soup of mist.
Silence. Nothing passes but the brokers, on their way
somewhere. One stopped, just now. Eyes came down from a
distance to my coat. I hurried on before he saw my face.

Everything's a tower round here. And most are dark.
But this is where he said to go, if I trusted him.
Smoky fingers, creeping out of manholes, stroke my trousers,
Streetlights stammer. Plywood windows yawn,
And there, on the corner, a statue on a dark plinth,
And writ, in aerosol: Roland Woz Ere.

Sweet Nothings to a Neighbourhood

by JILLIAN ADEL

I sit at the corner of 10 years of trying,
10 years of coffee shop hopeful dedicated heart
doing her best.
I sit on the street at Sunset darkening the lies
of a Capricorn Pluto,
bones born of hustle culture.

The sound of chats over diner omelette,
over mediocre overpriced pizza,
over millennial dreams drowned out
by the clang of corporate construction,
traffic jams,
rent that breaks our backs
and our bank accounts, big branding
and shitty murals approved in a board room
making my eyes bleed.

I believed in us, in all of us.
These corners morphing into strange lands,
and me with it, the structure of possibility with it.
I am here, but I feel like I've been spit out.

Lick me up again. Make me out.
Show me this decade meant something to you.
Be my land lover,
because I can't tell the truth.
And I'm on this corner 10 years
speaking sweet nothings to an empty room.

The Marketplace

by KALI JOY CRAMER

He confiscated doves
returned pigeons to the air
flipped tables like coins
in the hands of thieves
broke a sweat
shouldering the gates
to free a storm of animals
cursed traders caught
stripping the poor
to fund their own salvation

Arithmetical Anathema

by R. GERRY FABIAN

I receive the email
the profits are down
and there will be
no quarterly bonus.
They want me out.
All my top sales people
have gradually
been reassigned
and I've been given
the latest hires
who have no sale contacts.
I call a team meeting.
The fifteen plaques
on my office wall
as top salesman of the year
confirm,
I still have a multitude of contacts
and these computer savvy people
want to make money.

Dreams of the universe

by CHARLOTTE RENNER

We are custodial bodies
cleaning our cages and turning the clocks.
Our arms, often up, and waving
or down, and grovelling.
Our reflections in screens, and car windows.

These inventions we made,
our invention by land. Land's creation
by dust, dust's conception by weight.
We are always the thing, taking care of itself.

Reading the time for the first minute,
speeding towards a dial that we built.
A posit of our image, that gnomon.
The sun, our translator of light.

Space does not always permit you,
but it prompts you
to move away from where you came.
When we return to some core,
there won't be much else to do
but push out.

Wilshire Blvd.

by CHARLOTTE RENNER

It's been hours of the construction man,
donned in highlighter yellow and a hardhat,
walking up and down the alley
with his stop sign.
He walks out to instruct the traffic
so that the bulldozer can push a sheet of metal
and wood, then he walks
back into the alley behind it,
waiting for the signal to move out again.
Perhaps the myth of Sisyphus was
really just about man and his plight
of work on earth. The work
that seemingly never ends.
The hill, a poured block of asphalt,
and the boulder a laboured breath.

Sandwich Board, Soapbox & Bell

by MELANIE MCKERCHAR

Tethered by tentacles of over refined oil
the monster lurches and howls
soliloquy screeches from it
the black from the heart of the earth crawls up paws and claws
perched on void inside void inside void
it breaths black
fragile perch
clear coated strings of plastic
plastic streams
plastic ~~screams~~ screens
they say it is protection
handle with care
the beast tears
unpacks void upon void upon void
empty spaces created by our hands

I kneel	<every day 300 species go extinct>
hand in void	<every day 300 species go extinct>
knees ache	<every day 300 species go extinct>
we all kneel	<every day 300 species go extinct>
hand in void	<every day 300 species go extinct>

plastic gyre
mycelium pulsates

                    we made this
          heads inward   peril
        heads inward   perverse beauty
          heads inward   <><><><><>   enthralling dance
        heads inward   we laugh in fear circle of 14
                  a secret for lovers

CAPITALISM IS A DEATH CULT

        heads inward

megaflora fauna	dance	
pieces float down		twitch
heads outward		danger
feet to grass		abject
heads outward		
grass rising		
heads outward		
warm bodies		dance
hold me in place	twitch	
heads outward		danger
blades raise		abject

    we are such absurd puppets
    who is pulling the strings
        <><><><><>

A Hymn for the Faithful

by MELANIE MCKERCHAR

Oh these towers
crush
in stratification layers
oh these towers
pierce
pull
suck
fuck the dirt
into this glorious beast
/bitch/being/biology
omnipresent
as in the sea
as in the sky
as in the dirt
as in the flesh
divinity touching all
so it must become

Oh these towers
break
crack
decompose
drift
recompose
symbiotic networks we cast off
moving under every thoroughfare
spores in our voids
tangle dendrites seeking familiar,
familial, liminal ends, tangle
touch all
as in the sea
as in the sky

as in the dirt
as in the flesh
divinity touching all
so it must become

Oh these tunnels
divinus
trace your heavenly tracks
divinitas
grow fecund with our incessant
whispered worship
divinite
let us lie in the groves and grooves
of your heavy passing divine
Oh these mountains
let us feed you trash mother
workers scurrying
everywhere
as in the sea
as in the dirt
as in the flesh
so divinity rises
waste is wonder
drink from this void
be complete

The Amaltaas is in Bloom

by SHARJEEL H. TIWANA

It is spring again

the sun is warmer and the air moves slow
my favourite birds are all out singing
and speckled with clouds,
crawling out of a damp winter,
the sky is as pretty as it wills

It is spring again

the *kachnar* and the *jacaranda* are vibrant
and the *amaltaas* is bright yellow in bloom
and another poor man's house
my generous state has doomed

It is spring again

the soundtrack to my utopian city
are the gears of bulldozers and heavy machinery
ripping up the tin roofs
bringing down the patchwork walls
for we must make space
for one more glorious freeway
and one more grand avenue
but never mind all that my friend,
let us enjoy the flowers
after all there are no gardens in the slums

It is spring again

the Law is at its finest
and Order has never before been so perfect

CAPITALISM IS A DEATH CULT

let's enjoy the flowers,
as we watch the half dozen living
in that single room
their last ounce of dignity,
our generous state has doomed

It is spring again

the *kachnar* and the *jacaranda* are vibrant
and the *amaltaas* is bright yellow in bloom

and another poor man's house

my generous state has doomed.

20% off headstones all weekend!

by B.C. PELLEGRINI

they were dying yesterday and they are dying today
should we be grateful or angry
that the bombs changed colour?

empty promises
are stealing all the oxygen
while the wildfires keep spreading

we were dying yesterday and we are dying today
the air enters our lungs polluted
the water tastes metallic

useless words
useless gadgets
wasted time

we were dying yesterday and we are dying today
if you can't feed the machine
you may already be dead

rainbow shirts
pink and green
red and blue

we were dying yesterday and we are dying today
they keep telling us it's better
when the murderer looks like you

but the name doesn't matter
the colours mix
until they're the same

CAPITALISM IS A DEATH CULT

we were dying yesterday and we are dying today
the walls are closing in
they don't want us to exist

strike a match
burn it down
end it all to rebuild it

maybe we're already dead
maybe this is purgatory
or maybe it's just hell

our only way
to redemption
is to give it all back.

(death to) celebrity worship
by B.C. PELLEGRINI

they don't care:

that their jets are killing the planet
that their money could end poverty
that their word could sway millions
that they stole from minorities
that they're moulding young minds
that they're hoarding all wealth

that they could influence history
that they could influence politics
that they could stop bombs
that they could stop hunger
that they could do so much more
than performative charity

that people are starving
that people are dying
that people are people
not just numbers
streaming their songs
watching their movies
lining their pockets

Can I Please have the Floor?
by SAM HUANG

spent so long climbing up this endless
flights of stairs that I wasn't present
for the birth of my first-born daughter.
made it so high up that I had vertigo from
the sheer force of my own power until I
demolished the ceiling and broken glass
scarred my weary arms.

while he rides the elevator of mediocrity
all the way to the top floor, a penthouse suite
patiently waiting for his majesty,
my blood dribbles down the windows just as he
walks in and passively watches me, woozy
from natural loss, slip off the balcony,
once again entering the vast unknown.

sorry for writing so many poems
about catastrophically falling from great heights —
I just don't know how to cope with
losing a gorgeous perspective promised by
success.

O'Brien

by FREDERICK POLLACK

O'Brien, Winston's torturer
in *1984*, is disappointed
at how things have turned out.
He had felt a certain pride
in the Book (Bernstein's book) he had
ghostwritten, and
a bond with the ghosts it was written for.
That world had had an elegance, a logic.
This one, individualistic through
and through, confuses power
with sadism, which is not the same thing,
is even the opposite thing. Proles, of course,
remain proles, but the masters are idiots:
they enjoy their yachts and nymphets,
their lies remain mere lies. The religions
alone show something
of the proper spirit, but convulsive,
wasteful. He has met Trump twice,
found him easy to deal with,
looks mildly forward to a second term.
Sits meanwhile in a tasteful suit and surroundings,
greying, distinguished,
approached by those with a need to know
where bodies are buried.

Bite the Rich

by SARAH GAWTHROP

If rest is radical
then the slow slump to success
is a merciless beast.
Give me moss-covered understory
and little babbling brooks,
give me mycelium networks
over network networks every damn day.
You eat your cake
and take your neighbour's too,
drain the vital marsh,
shove your greed-plugged pate
in the fertile aftermath,
strip the DRC of cobalt
for your widgets,
your ephemeral pleasures.
I take your bitcoin
and bite you with teeth
that cut through wildflowers—
make a daisy crown instead.
Softly, slowly, I split the stem
Thread one through another,
place it on my lover's head,
fall back to Earth
who loves me, even though
I betray her
every
damn
day.

Job Hunting

by SARAH BLAKELY

I'm on the prowl, creeping low
to the barren ground,
hunting quietly, preying piously
for a job that puts food on the table.

My careful camouflage makes me fairly invisible -
I blend into the herd of hunters,
but I don't stand out enough to compete
with these out-for-blood hounds.
I've got no experience, I'm not trained
to shoot this shotgun in my helpless hands
that tremble,
so guide my unskilled fingers –
walk me through the kill.

Teach me the way of the interview,
how to shapeshift
into the creature I seek, adopt their habits
and mimic their call until I can speak
their language,
reciting what they want to hear.
Show me how to lock in my aim,
how to pull the trigger
when opportunity presents itself.
A confident and firm handshake
to close the deal,

a binding ink signature claiming the life
I've been training for.
I'll pierce the skin with my pen,
reach inside, remove
the heart with its love and wanting,
the lungs, gasping for freedom,
the liver and its resilience to heal,
the stomach that hungers endlessly,
the womb and all its potential.

Carve away at this body until
it is a hollow carcass
of strong bones, tender meat,
and muscles defined
by carrying the weight of the economy
on its burdened and aching shoulders.
This lifeless creature I've become to survive
is bleeding out before my eyes
and the predators will continue feasting
on my body
until even the scavengers find nothing left
to pick away at.

Uncommitted

by JORDON BRIGGS

I've sustained democracy
with my fingertips
every cycle, the duty's ache returns,
filling up the oval
my belief leaving
the pen hot.
For a long time
casting hope onto them
cooled me
more than the breeze
flowing during voting day sunsets.
I always honor our agreement:
I pick them, they'd accomplish those bedrock dreams
implement those self evident truths we both share.
Yet
They
remain uncommitted
to their promise.
Before we made it official
I spoke of barriers—they absorbed my story,
became my voice,
designated me partner.
We would embody the completion
of the project called freedom.

They
remain uncommitted
to consider how our future remains
a vision, year after year after
They
desert or deny full forgiveness of student debt—

defect from or dismiss increasing
the federal minimum wage
forcing me to vote between saving or staying afloat;
demobilize strikes
launched on designated double shifts
derailing time to devour meals with loved ones,
depriving me of time with myself to dream.
They pervade me
with a word from our promise: partner
holding only me to my end
of our bargain.

I've honored the ancestors
ballot marks   not bullets   delivered
my voice   enough violence   for a change
I was taught
to believe that through the power of
Them
will the barriers to a future disappear.
They were given the same lesson
and lived by it until they became
Them
and I ponder on what happened to my partner.
Maybe they too chose to dance with devils they know.
They conceal if this is true, yet I witness
both our bodies grow weaker
stiffer, then subdued
as we perform those hand-me-down moves
trying to keep up.

They
remain uncommitted
to consider how, when
They claim I'm vulnerable to our enemies,
my focus racks
to differences between me and my neighbors,

in person   online   in my mind
      ID'ing myself
and others
with colors
confirming sides.
As my second gig becomes keeping receipts
my body recalls my dream for me:
all in our union experiencing adequate life,
never treated differently than another.
These scenes help me breathe—
reform
  absorb identical struggles
    socialize   authenticate my needs
I direct my representative to the unrealized—
but I mind the roar rushing from my savior
when there are bills handled, temporary raises
enemy language banned or canceled.
Their words secure me
so I elect to remain home.

They
remain uncommitted
though, to re-adjust
Their priorities,
unconcerned with how raised taxes
tax,
generating defeat in my spirit
restricting resurrection from deficit,
while relief transfers to traders.
They tell me to see the bigger picture
like in the Declaration:"mankind is disposed to suffer"—
to pull myself up by my busted boot straps to
Their position,
and dance to our anthem with
Them tonight.

CAPITALISM IS A DEATH CULT

I honor us
dreading voicelessness
dreading villainy
dreading who I am: peacemaker.
I sustain the double shift—
in bed, I plead with my thoughts for time off,
my body still tasked, works
towards retirement,
my inner world tethered to the unfulfilled.
Somehow, somewhere in me I must believe
They know something I don't.

They
remain uncommitted
to reexamine our dynamic.
No acknowledgment of my hurt when
They exclude my voice.
No acknowledgment of my toil to defend
my role to loved ones.
No acknowledgment of my spirit's turmoil
to remain loyal.
They
remain uncommitted
to come back home—
to lower the cost of my care.

They
remain uncommitted
to consider that freedom is not sole pursuits,
but closing the gap between us.

They
remain uncommitted
to examine
Their dread
to appear vulnerable

Sunday Mornings at the River

that created
concentration camps
for Oakland's Japanese community,
now, claim to their Town exists as an idea—
created the Vietnamese refugee
refining Houston's economy,
stuck in the gear of survival,
created the displaced Ukrainian
applying for discounts on phone and internet,
submitting an EBT card as proof of disparity—
created surveillance on the Palestinian in New York,
their story with their abuser
obscured on major news.
They
remain uncommitted to engage with
the lingering injury of the young—the experienced
—and the elder organizing
to end war.

They
remain uncommitted
to repair.
They
remain uncommitted
to prevent my invalidation
when a manager determines for me,
that I haven't experienced
discrimination based on my brown skin,
when I'm the only one of my color undermined
by daily dismissers
who later claim they did not accept my contributions,
because I don't smile enough
beneath the mask all employees are required to wear.

They
remain uncommitted

to transforming the system of survival
that created my dire need to believe
that at my next job
color won't matter;
remain uncommitted
to consider the weight of being
my only resource for staying alive.

I wander around wondering if I matter.
I doubt my dream will materialize.
My body unbinds my weight through tears.
No ancestors to rebel with me.
Having honored our binary system
I cling to the pieces of me leftover.

In my mind   online   in person
I quote the Declaration
I "demand an alteration,
demand we lay new foundation."
I bring them to the table, they inflate achievements,
dismiss the harm, offer no remedy
for how I worked towards our dream, alone.
Working unto themselves,
they've abandoned our plan for our future.

They
don't see me as their partner.
They
don't see me as someone to know intimately.
They
don't want to hear the desires I keep close anymore.
They
don't want to share their inner world with me
and help guide each other to achieve our goal—
The project of freedom.

Sunday Mornings at the River

They
remain uncommitted
to our previous procedures, electing themselves
as the parent, eliminating any possible threat,
any possible experience.

They
remain uncommitted
to the right to choose.

I know, now, that I am unwanted
in their vision for us.
They've made me homeless.
I let out tears over the truth that I meant nothing
and never will to
Them.

They
remain uncommitted
to the promise to simply commit.

They
remained uncommitted
to us.

So I will leave, and unlearn the dance,
unlearn the steps, unlearn the belief I have to dance at all—
unlearn what I was taught to get my needs met, and then
relearn from my choices,
remaining committed to my future self.

They Were Once Real

by GIORGIA CIPOLLONI

Machine men all over the place.
Machine men providing bleeding for profit,
Machine men forcing machine men into machine men.
Machine men murdering the arts,
the analogue, my typewriter, my uncle's camera.
Machine men recording the moments
they forgot to live.
Machine men turning children into machine men;
Machine men alone.
Machine men individualized,
Machine men alienated,
Machine men depressed,
Machine men obsessed,
repressed,
by the very same system they created,
and were once
created
for.
Machine men, the new God.
Machine men profiting from genocide, rape, war.
Machine men without identity,
for knowing who you are
requires awareness,
which they lack.
Machine men do not recognize
who they're sharing a table with;
Machine men do not know.
Machine men alone.

Auschwitz by the Sea

by STEVE DUNN

Displaced by 80,000 tonnes of bombs
the structures, and the people
seek out shelter, memories
amongst crushed, deserted dust
swarm of human rubble
thousands dead and missing
used for target practice
arms race progress
multi billion dollar success
overwhelms a desperate struggle
people are thin, dogs are fat
obstructions to a vision
expulsion to pop up reservations
scattered to indifferent lands
no protective western bubble
paradise from planned pain
Auschwitz by the sea
check in any time you like
but you can never grieve
human standard double
forced exodus of tortured souls
poverty knows no borders
problem solved with dollars
contracts flow for super cleansing
ranting orange psycho babble

Umbrella Men

by RACHAN

beware the umbrella men,
black suits, black cars, black ties and
eyes, pale arms stained with black ink and
hidden blood, dark smiles
behind closed doors, fake smiles
in front of cameras,
thin membrane s t r e t c h e d
over sharp spines of steel,
the appearance of
size without substance,
dark threatening presence
larger than life,
dark heralds of the
oncoming storm,
untouched by the deluge,
beware walking in a crowd of
umbrella men, black
umbrellas held high to
hide from the rain,
at least on the surface, but
below to hide from lies
locked in obsidian blocks,
umbrellas closed into weapons to duel,
dual shield and sword
neither used for what it
should be, both used to ward
off questions and cases and allegations,

Sunday Mornings at the River

black shoes stepping on you,
black briefcases pushing too
many people out the way
on the way to offices full of
black ink on white paper,
ripping lives, countries, earth
apart with black pens,
umbrella men
shaping umbrellas and words into
weapons, heed the pen,
mightier than the sword,
but beware more the umbrella,
and the man who wields it.

Necro Scene

by PAUL ATTEN ASH

Unnoticed, a grim ghost creeps in,
silently through the pale garden,
to lie down by us all, and we feel it

like a cloud has passed across the sun

but tomorrow we'll raise a glass to
a blind, spindrift angel of history,
drinking in the wreckage piling up

while next to our head it holds a gun

it's the slow-blackening of the soul,
plastic-wrapped and air-freighted,
Black Friday like some new religion

working its way into children's bones

born bloodless, solivagant spectres,
bastard runts of our oil-rich kin,
hours beating the razed forest paths

to witness the world bleed out, alone.

Prayer for Giving Up Shopping on Amazon

by RUTH LEXTON

Am I not enough? For I see you
smiling as I relinquish
my time and surrender to
the commodification of labour.

Send me forbearance –
because you know how to hurt me:
exactly where to place the knife
and what I will do when you twist it.

Deliver me strength of mind –
because you know what I am hungry for
and what it feels like to withhold it.
And what it feels like to take it.

Return me equanimity –
because giving should not be convenient.
And happiness is not a window vacuum
that is also a window cleaner that requires
monthly refills.

Redeem my instincts –
because bigger
          better
                  faster
                          more
will not bestow clarity or energy
or love or fill up the emptiness:
not every problem can be solved
by buying a thing.

CAPITALISM IS A DEATH CULT

Offer me your mercy –
because you know the name
and birthdate and address
of my firstborn child.
Because if you can sell it, you will.
Because when you said
that I said it's what I wanted,
you know that's not what I meant.

Now let me have quietude. For I know that
saving money is an illusion and need is relative.
Besides, I don't know about you
but I feel like the world is ending often and soon.
And I've already paid, Bezos.

The Cabin

by VIOLA LEE

Sometimes, my life reminds me of a cabin
made of cedar and planks of three-by-fours.
On occasion, there are poems;
friends to visit to say they have to pee,
music and guitars playing
singing simple songs of plain melody.
The walls are covered in coloured pencil drawings
and sculptures hanging made of leaf, yarn,
stick, and air. Sometimes, my life
reminds me of a cabin
with ants and pinecones,
a broken porch,
to remind me of the stars, the cosmos,
and these unforgiving heavens.
And it's all temporary light,
it's all temporary light you see,
the existence of being in the world,
of the world, *universal respect,*
my art teacher once said to me,
where nothing takes,
and where nothing is achieved.

The Borders

by VIOLA LEE

the borders are the people who make our food who build our houses and craft our clothes. the borders supply the materials for the buildings where we labour and give birth in. the borders are the people who make our rugs make the wires that keep our homes full of warmth the borders are those who care for our families who teach our children to read who make our scripts that keep us entertained who build our stages and costumes and designers of our backdrops. the borders are those who take our blood pressure and construct our pills and tea. the borders plant our food and freeze our seeds protect our streets give care to our parents and grandparents and families. the borders create our poems and make new words. the borders are our lawyers that work to justify. the borders who also say, order, to become all of our judges and our water advocates. the borders are our jugglers and nurses, rug makers and food scientists. the borders have sent us to the moon. the borders are the tariffs made of metal made of sterling silver spoons.

I Hear the Birds Screech Like Loose Hinges

by VARINA DRAGO

October, I'm drugging the birds out of me.
Their pitch black voices brick-slam the pavements,
crunch like skulls
opening scuffs in windows.
Morning arrives entrepreneurially
early, zombie-tinged in business attire
grey which gradually
autocorrects to blue-eyed skies
and blonde sun formulaic
as Nazi offspring propaganda.
I push out the thought.
I'm getting worse like the news.
Feelings are scattered,
left on park benches as decaying tributes,
carved into trunks
growing stabbed initials and forever's slackening into
homes
hollow with tree ants. This country serves up disaster silver-
plated with profits. The air has a list of ingredients
longer than faux eggs I buy in protest of chickens
debeaked and fleshed with antibiotics. My mood an inflated
rubber tyre penduluming back and forth, never taking off
from its incubation nest. The flowers are censored by
politics. Days soon dark as alleys short-circuiting to
evening. The year feels like a grudge that will never let go.
Summer is experiencing some delays. Flight of migratory

birds has crashed like Wall Street. Our blood sugar dope-high, screen time non-refundable. Rain drips like a voice thick with sarcasm. Sky stripped of its sunny merchandise that says falsely, everything will be okay. And I want to blurt out tears.

The Children's United of Nation

by ROBERT FREDE KENTER

What does the dark say and how does it feed me?
Swallowing sticky syrup in blood and
viscous light,
I see you at the top of the hill,
contracting for the framework of my house,
bidding to tug out nails and hammer
them back in
to the side of my head, leaving me with
scars and sores
that pulse, *with which I sing, would you pull me even closer.*

Tracing hand over hand along
the line of ligaments.
To frame the ligature of stars embossed in spores
in the dust of the road
and the dark bread basket of the nation.

Preparing and ironing the suits
of the damned milliners,
digging holes everywhere and parting and
crying into cocktail party hats and
handkerchiefs, of all the widows-to-be
in black crepe,
the silk hats of their husbands' dead hands
folded at their belts and
the multi-billion dollar combines,
great-coat buttons
cascading down the geese-filled sky,
flying saucers in a children's confetti parade,
replete with flags.

CAPITALISM IS A DEATH CULT

Skittering cacophony of shouting
from a graffiti-drawn sarcophagus
of coughing junkies,
 all my brothers and sisters in the phlegm
 of aggrieved nations!

Part the curtains, peer out from bay windows
into cold ocean plastic, plasma poems
of the ocean,
suffocate and flutter in eyelashes,
as if a million water droplets in a hurricane wind
could rise up and dance,
not unlike the million crystals of the brutal shards
of night-demon skeletons in suitcoats
and top hats that tap-dance,
all Gene Kelley, Fred Astaire and Ginger Rogers.

Brittle bristling barristers,
paper weights affixed to the eye sockets
of twilight, eyeing
horizons of endless white paper
blank and sticky
flying through the
bleeding burning sky.

Streamers oozing in granulated crusts
of mourner's tears, until everything that dies
dries in the dust of final leave-taking.

The breakfast ruse   the residue of honey
and buzzing bees.
Aviators in military formation.

And we ask one another, *where shall we eat?*
What to eat next?

Cyclones, funnels, tornado laneways,

stalled, disintegrated, disinterested, disinterred
automobiles.

Sliding down a saccharine, sanctimonious,
steep graveyard hill, knowing every white-picket
fence post lies angled beyond the low rent
Tombstone Towers.

Territorial
by VIKKI C.

I tell him the world is a terrible thing to own. A desert powders and expands around the radius of rescue.

The hospital itself becomes a borderline case. Elsewhere, a neighbour aggravates the plot—because power is

complicated, depending where you fall or lie, and how a boundary obscures under a corruption of

milkweed. Power too, can be delicate in your hands, laid beside a lover, breath travelling down the spine, like

driving the mundane Pacific coast which was never man-made, but the sea's rage taking back a little of our

land-locked problems. So many endangered things are taken to heart— down this fine divide between

intimacy and survival. "We haven't the tools to cultivate who we were," says a mother carrying two babies of

different lineage. Their legs dangling from her hips, next to a hunting blade. Grief is a regional aspect turned

away from the sun. The lines on a palm say a hand is most blessed without a ring. And the mouth and heart

sometimes align to form a crossing, free from the weight of their machines.

Crane Ballet

by JOHN O'HARE

just another test,
going round in circles,
performing pirouettes,
amongst industrial ruins,
their skeletal frames at full stretch,
like ladders of failure,
swinging empty payloads,
bony arms and big fists,
groaning like lonely dinosaurs,
unwanted reminders of enterprise,
and of being useful,
then they are put to rest,
awkwardly folded,
bowing to no one.

A Visit to the Dentist

by MALAVIKA SURESH

CAPITALISM asked me why my teeth
were bleeding today,
hands me a tissue made from someone else's skin.

In this sterile dentist's office,
I lay reclined with my mouth to the sky,
silence and blood pooling in my throat.

CAPITALISM stands above me,
drill embedded in my tongue,
asks again why I am bleeding.

Through metallic teeth and lips, I smile,
wincing, and say—
You are so kind for allowing me to barely survive.

Corporations Don't Need Passports

by SEAN POWER

Build a wall 'round Walmart. The slow trickle
of sales back to mom
and pop stores. Foreign? Walmart
and other corps wink
at the Chinese origin of their American flags.

From deep space,
the eyes of border hysteria burn.
Face offs between blood-shot border guards,
fences trimmed with razor wire, footsteps
in the sand where migrants lost their way—
all fade.

Breath migrates, as does blood.
Movement—the pulse
of life. For those Africans who follow
hominids' footsteps out of the continent
and beyond, the stares
close in as tight as walls.

Us and them. Skin colour, language, stars
made of felt all mark the "other." The orbit
of fear. A forgetfulness
that we share one another's breath.

Polar bears enter cities due to shrinking ice cover.
Paltry corn harvests in Guatemala tug children out of bed.

CAPITALISM IS A DEATH CULT

Stars flutter like Monarchs to guide them northwards.
Walmart opens its doors—nylon tents
for border camping, made in China.

Elon spent hours in space but orbits
greed. Mexicans block Central Americans
from their line in the dirt. Walmart can keep selling
its American flags, no passport required and under
the logo of a yellow star.

That's maybe the problem: consciousness
doesn't have a corporate PR team, a sky-blue
colour pattern, or a catchy slogan. Always low prices.

Never enough.

White Mail

by SEAN POWER

White mail, the standard. White male,
deviates. I pray to never go postal
like so many other white men and teens.
Paper thin psyches, set to tear
at the smallest perceived slight.

White men fight to preserve the standard.
The white man at the top,
even the notion of making
space for others: a free
fall. Hold on or die, they say.
And label everyone else as deviants.

The Lone Ranger withers on the vine
of aging—elder white men having
among the highest suicide rates. Paper thin
resilience, unlike that of Black women
who the US Veterans Administration studied
to learn about their quilt
of social ties.

I know better than to mansplay
or choose a crowd
to spray with indignation. But I relent.
Men like me stare
back from the currency and I can forget
that "danger" has been stamped

on those of a darker complexion.

In my stomach I sense the loss.
The yearning for connection, particularly with Blacks:
those I have been taught to fear.
I want to shed this itchy sweater. And yet,
what am I willing to give up, to pay it forward
for the wealth that has been stolen
in the first place?

Society pays for this invisible sickness.
He seemed fascinated with guns,
they might say of another white man gone wild.
Rare is the profile
made clear, that white men are a national terror,
white-robed or not.

White male, how to break this standard?
This path that burdens us all
and our planet.
The myth of our grandeur ensures
our erasure as a species. Is this a standard
to bear?

I am not hopeful.
White men devour possibility to save
delusions of providence.
And our supposed proximity
to the sun. Silly fools,
we are too focused on the rays
to realize we are lost. Even harder to swallow:

we need those "beneath" us to find a way home.

White men, the choice is ours.
We will make mistakes.
We will step on shadows we fear.
But, there is no other way to break the standard
than through our every action, and deviate,
deviate, deviate.

CAPITALISM IS A DEATH CULT

From Some Hell

by LEAH KEANE

From the motorway balcony
in my bus palace
I see a garden in full bloom.
How beautifully we're infested
with every shade of green.
There's a dip in our landscape.
The sun infiltrates.
When will you understand?
It doesn't shine for any of us.

How now will any a cow
be more than grazing shadow
when forests worldwide
are hosting barbeques
and toasting us with them?
Once in the midst of our charred remains,
exactly whose bones will you be licking?

With all due respect,
those Hindus have it right.
We should love our beef.

But dear God, do we love our beef.
Wrapped in forty layers of plastic.
And isn't it earth shatteringly funny how
so many people still don't know yet?

Still, I bet you'll love it.
The slapstick humour
of everyone around you
not being able to breathe
for some unknown reason.

Sunday Mornings at the River

Won't you laugh until you're dead?

But first you'll blame Jesus.
I want you to feel how heavy beauty is
on the verge of total destruction.

And I hope that from some hell
you get to watch your babies drown.

And Then You Think

by CHRIS BUTTERS

It's like voting
for Republicans
year after year
and never making the connection

it 's like growing up in Lake Hiawatha
where the Indians were killed off
the polluted lake bulldozed
long ago

it's like wondering
if Peace for Galilee
means the invasion of Lebanon
how come making love isn't genocide

it's like the moon and the stars
as you say goodbye to your friend
and then head home to
separate ghettoes

if it costs the same
to send a kid to prison as to college
its like asking why the kid can't
just be sent to college

its's like the glitter of the rich
buying Maserati's
and the sound of the nothingness
trickling down

it's like a benefit
for breast cancer research

sponsored by your dear friends
at the Dow Chemical Company

It's like a war
from the folks
who brought you the war
to end all wars

It's like watching
the news one night
amid the speedup, cutbacks,
layoffs of your life

then stumbling upon
the candidates debate:

"I'm running for President
because I believe
with strong leadership
America's glorious days

will always lie ahead of us,
just as they lie
ahead of us now….."

the way things sound,
round and serious,
smooth and deep

and then
you think —

(previously published in Blue Collar Review)

The Midnight Zone

by LEWIS WYN DAVIES

I missed out
on the big tickets
this morning
so I've been trying
to make myself
more noticeable
in the world
I've searched
and scrolled
followed
and liked
dived deeper
and deeper
into the dregs
of websites
waded through
the backwash
of apps
gone
        down
                down
                        down
                down
        down
photos
captions
and blue ticks
have blurred by
I've been given
suggestions
for many new names
to connect with

the algorithm thinks
I should try
the Washington post
it's flashing
their reel about
the midnight zone
across my timeline
a part of the ocean
that even the sun's
fingertips
can't reach
the only light
being self-made
by the zone's own
inhabitants
and I imagine
all the unseen
looking for guidance
in the darkness
they were born in
as a sudden chill
sinks through me
I think I've always been here

The Anatomy of Capitalism

by KAZI RAIDAH AFIA NUSAIBA

"Capitalism is religion. Banks are churches. Bankers are priests.
Wealth is heaven. Poverty is hell. Rich people are saints.
Poor people are sinners. Commodities are blessings. Money is God."
                                            -Miguel D. Lewis

The false god watches from billboards and screens
ten-faced Argus with eyes that never close
each iris an algorithm tracking our devotion
each pupil dilating at the scent of our desperation

scrolling through feeds of
bodies in Gaza
bodies at borders
bodies in detention
bodies in flood waters
bodies in factory collapse
the god offers no salvation, only an ad for anxiety medication
nestled between corpses. tap to shop.

See this deity demands constant penance
whispers through every channel:
"you're not working hard enough"
"you're not thin enough"
"you're not straight enough"
"you're not white enough"
"you're not abled enough"
"you're not male enough"
"you're not rich enough"
"you're not enough"

we pray with bloodied fingers on keyboards

sacrifice sleep to digital altars
tithe our data to algorithmic priests
in the cathedral of capital,
spent cartridges serve as rosary beads
Money written on brass
that penetrated healthcare
Greed etched on casings
that tore through climate science
Power stamped on bullets
that silenced whistleblowers

the insurance adjusters, modern-day inquisitors
calculating which heretics deserve healing
which sinners must suffer
which sacrifices please the market

I watch my trans friend weep
at the pharmacy counter
another communion denied
by corporate scripture
while rainbow logos flicker like stained glass
in June's performative light

the congressman delivers last rites
—"thoughts and prayers"—
over child-sized coffins
his pockets heavy with offerings
from the gun lobby
the corporation genuflects toward Palestine
while its machinery levels homes in Gaza
baptizing civilians in rubble

this is transubstantiation for the modern age:
hypocrisy becomes virtue
violence becomes peace
exploitation becomes opportunity

CAPITALISM IS A DEATH CULT

"What are you even talking about?" You ask me

remember that scene in Parasite?
the rich family's lawn floods
while the poor family drowns in their basement

this is not metaphor anymore—this is prophecy

the pollution flows downstream like holy water
blessing neighbourhoods by property value
by melanin concentration
by historical redlining maps

the factory waste seeps into soil
like communion wine
"we can't afford environmental regulations"
declares the high priest with three homes
his children drink water flown from Fiji
untainted by his divine industrial runoff

Haha in this church, the disabled body kneels
in constant apology
for disrupting the sacred efficiency
for needing accommodation
for existing outside the canon of productivity

the fat body performs penance
for occupying space in the temple of thinness
for refusing the sacrament of starvation
for the mortal sin of self-acceptance

women's bodies become sacrificial vessels
consent an outdated ritual
replaced by the modern doctrine
of ownership disguised as desire

Black bodies bear the stigmata

of systemic violence
then face excommunication for bleeding
while shallow fascism preaches from Silicon Valley
pulpits wearing Patagonia vestments and preaching
prosperity gospel via TED talks

You see our new clergy doesn't need jackboots
or crosses
it has terms of service agreements
privacy policies no one reads
customer service holds that last forever
paperwork that multiplies
like biblical loaves and fishes

how many indigenous children
in unmarked graves
before the pope renounces manifest destiny?

how many Black bodies in privatized prisons
before we admit the plantation was outsourced,
not abolished?

how many "me toos" before we recognize
rape culture as the oldest liturgy?

how many queer kids driven to suicide
before conversion therapy joins
the index of torture?

how many Palestinians buried in rubble
before we question our tithe
to the promised land?

these are not rhetorical questions
these are the stations of the cross
in the religion of capital

CAPITALISM IS A DEATH CULT

BANISH the False God
BURN their loyal followers
BREAK their Brick temples that they call Marble
this trinity keeps the faith
ensures the doctrine remains unchallenged
the congregation docile
the collection plates full

"We need the money for the good and the needy." You say.

But I walk past the unhoused man everyday
his cardboard sign a heretical text
challenging everything in the capitalist bible
about merit
about work
about salvation through consumption

the priest in their expensive suit
declares him damned by choice
fallen through laziness
unworthy of sanctuary

the congregation averts their eyes
drops coins like indulgences
absolving themselves of complicity

tbh the matrix wasn't sci-fi
it was documentary
we're all just batteries now
powering a system that consumes us
and half of y'all would still swallow
the blue pill if offered
 Our familiar hell over uncertain freedom
 #justfalsegodsthingsIguess

"So...what exactly are you saying?
Be direct." You say to me

Sunday Mornings at the River

My child, in the communion of capital
we eat the wafer of minimum wage
drink the wine of student debt
confess our sins of poverty
tithe our labour to billionaires
pray for healthcare that won't bankrupt us
worship at the altar of productivity
fear the hell of homelessness
hope for the heaven of retirement
that recedes like a mirage

while the ten-faced god watches
as we turn against each other
blaming immigrants
blaming welfare recipients
blaming anyone but the priests
who count their money
behind golden doors
The money of the ordinary,
piled up like dirty laundry
around the corner.
the spent cartridges pile up around the altar
"Oh and by the way", you all sheep say
"the unholy trinity of late-stage capitalism
blessed be thy shareholder value
thy profit come
on earth as it is
in offshore accounts"
Oh heavens Oh heavens
what if we recognized this god as false?
all of us at once just stopped believing
what if we refused communion?
tore up the scripture of quarterly profits?
saw the god of money for what it
just paper
just metal
just digits on screen

CAPITALISM IS A DEATH CULT

just another golden calf

what if we named the unnameable?
pointed at the frauds?
took sides?
started arguments?
shaped the world?
stopped it from going to sleep?

this is apostasy, I know
but as Rushdie said—
that's what poets are for

The Illusion

by LEE SHERIDAN

Should you lead a life defined by gain,
you'll leave no room for loss, and with
loss comes space and holes and time that
you'll work to fill by the sweat of your brow.

With every spadeful of dirt – a teaspoon's worth
in the beach of eternity – you'll learn that dirt is
all it really is.

Give your wounds to the rain instead;
let that soak in and wash them clean.

You were before what you will be after –
nothing can be brought, though every cock
crows loudest atop his own dungheap.

You are a tenant like the rest of us,
no matter what you think you own.

To Be Pawns

by CLAIRE KROENING

Where is the empathy,
        the human decency?
Herded as lambs to slaughter
with every action dictated
by pigs proclaiming messiah,
high on ever-crackling power.

Where is the empathy,
        the human decency?
Invisible chains shackled to our necks
with the world hanging
in an unsteady balance,
holding what breaths we have left
for the first bombs to touch down.

There is no freedom—
replaced by high-tech cars,
slowly-fading papers
of a country brought upon its knees
by multi-billion thrones.

Is there any empathy
        remaining in humanity's disgrace?
Or is freedom reserved for the past;
        the wealthy?

Capitalism Dies in Decolonized Dreams

by SONYA SONI

My freedom fighter great-grandmother was jailed by
British empire for spinning *khadi*,
The women in my family all too familiar with the cold
touch of prison floors as the fertile soil of capitalist
earth. Our *zardosi*, *bandhani*, *kalamkari* textiles were our
protest signs The British East India Company could
never mass produce the handlooming embedded in
ancestral memory, Fourteen generations of *khaligars*
worth.

"Exile is when you live in one land and
dream in another," Iranian poet Abbas Milani
once wrote.

One generation later,
The descendents of my revolutionary ancestor eagerly
arrive on their colonizers' land.
My grandmother's ironed sari pleats stiff above the
bleached linoleum floors and under carceral
fluorescent lighting on the first day of her first job at
Heathrow Airport. I remember that same sari on my
great-grandmother, the way it danced and reflected
the hazy forgiving sun on jute-lined Delhi rooftops as
she braided jasmine into her freely wild hair.

CAPITALISM IS A DEATH CULT

Decades later, capitalist dreams lived on, floating across borders, across oceans.

Dada stares at Zee TV on a plastic-lined sofa in Orange County with glassy zombie eyes.
A shell of himself craves a pirated, digital copy of homeland. I imagine him yearning for the Bollywood song-and- dance entourage on the screen bought from hard-eared American dollars to teleport into the ghostly cookie cutter streets of his,
To combat eerily suburban silences with longing and aliveness.

In a cloud of recurring dreams, I ask my Dada over and over again, "Was it worth it to leave gods and hope and memory behind for this?"
I am too afraid to hear his regretful response met with tears, or even worse, a cheery, hope-stuffed lie.

At what point of desperation do we arrive at to abandon: Our ancestral whispers laced between sari pleats and raga beats?
Our starry monsoon skies that rain prayers and poems? For a possibility not guaranteed to us,
To believe in a canon that we can live equally alongside our captors who proved to us,
time and time again, we will never find belonging in a land birthed from our blood.

Sunday Mornings at the River

Under capitalist moons, we are made to feel our
homeland is never enough, we are never enough.
The walls of immigrant-stuffed factories remind me
of Jallianwallah Bhag's blood-stained ones
Farmer suicides in my homeland of Punjab mirror
those of Sikh taxi drivers in Queens.

How many childhoods of my ancestors died at the
feet of capitalist empire?
But there is no amount of migration across borders
and oceans to the mythical dreamscapes that capitalism
sells my ancestors that can extract the marigolds and
agarbathi and cardamom in our hair.

We are not meant to be
caged. We are birthed from:
The rhythms of the Dalit Panthers protests and
Mohammad Rafi's ghazals,
The mustard fields of Punjab that sprouted the largest
revolution in human history,
Kesari mangoes that will never be able to be mass
produced with Monsanto seeds,
Pre-partition maps and souls that are borderless,
Our Naani's almirahs, shelved with ikat, unstolen
indigo, and wild imagination,
Holy walls with the fiery spirit of Kali, *chardi kala*, &
Allah.

What if our collective memory turns
defiant? What if we traded in the
American dream for decolonized ones?

Fingers laced with aam juice and revolutions
dripping of *azadi*
What if we dissect the mythology of capitalist dreamscapes like a cadaver?
Let it bleed out like so many of our freedom fighters did.
Mock it, dehumanize it, smash it, like it did to us Unclothe the one who seduced us into colonial cages we never knew we were rotting in.

On Ambition
by KATE SMITH

a black tube returns creek to creek
and river otters splash
at its outlet a heron fishes
and more nest at the top of a grey
leafless tree I want that rush
and that height under a clear
sky and August sun
tell me it is not too much to ask for
my life measured in something other
than inches words
minutes deadlines emails bylines
followers pageviews
I want to splash messages
over rocks fish stories from this
shared water hold hands swim toward air
I want you to press your palm to my chest
invite love into my belly
invite me in too let me feel the heat
and pulse of my own
flesh alive under my fingers
and yours alive too too much
to demystify learn create
organize there is not enough time
which is why I want a portion of it back
so much I would feel
a sliver for rest and a sliver for imagination
a bit for me and an abundance for you these are our lives
we are not asking for too much

LinkedIn

by MATEO X

we were here for a moment,
and called it *the moon*. and we
toiled to keep our bellies
from shrieking, hauled by an
inexplicable appetition for
survival. and we gazed at the
firmament and declared it a
deity, anointing ourselves
with its powers. we drew lines
across the earth, demarcating our
love, squeezing blood from a
neighbour. chirping, twirling.
distended. and we trod teleological
trails, spooling cobwebs in our minds,
thread upon thread—weaving coarse
throws of assurances, draping them
over our shoulders, abrading
moisturized skin. and we forged
syndicates and concocted marketing
schemes, heaving up collateral—howling,
belching, contemplating birdsong. our
tongues foaming like slugs smothered in
salt—we charred our cities and
gnawed raw nipples in fragrant
apartments to the stabs of hi-hats and
kicks, forgetting, at times, to

bathe in the busy stillness of
evening gold and hover empty
under the disc of a
naked moon.

Humankind

by KATE GOUGH

If they don't already believe
they're in a dystopia,
they're either not paying attention
or they're one of the lucky ones.

An operatic melody
plays over rubble and ash.
They let the hate burn—
red, hot—
never once wondering
if maybe they are human too.

Death.
Decay.
The way they treat the vulnerable.
The sick.
The old.
It will all come back around.

As they listen to the final song,
the end draws near—
and so does the truth.

They want the truth to be kind?
When they can't even be kind
to each other?

Human kind,
incapable of seeing one another
as human kind.

One Week's Notice

by ROSE WINTER

Monday I turn in my notice, and the city slowly reveals itself to me again. Tuesday starts with the roads covered in a thin sheen of water—the world in reflection seems a more accurate version of what is coming up ahead. Wednesday is mauve light behind city hall as I leave work—violent I would almost say, but then it sounds like I have mistyped the word violet. Thursday now and I can't help but notice the cream-dappled leaves on the hedges pushing through King William Park's fence—they would be the envy of all the 'plant moms' who live in my Facebook feed. Friday comes and it goes.

Monday, and it feels like it actually will all be grand in the end, and not just because for dinner I have had two lychee martinis. Tuesday everyone at the pub quiz is asking how it feels to be done with the job and there isn't enough time to explain between the questions—the bonus round is called simply 'The Troubles' and the quizmaster cannot hide the acerbic edge to his voice. Wednesday the only thing I manage to do that fits into the category of 'my personal life' is screenshot the application link for a writers reality TV programme in Cusco which I know is a scam but might still be the game-changer I need. Thursday is a day to watch the entire last season of Derry Girls and wonder if it is fundamentally because of who I am as a person that I have quit my job but not been fully allowed to leave and now the weeks bleed together—but Friday is here again and it is Valentine's Day and I am told to take the back stairs fetching coffee for a client so they don't see how the coffee reaches them and I—

Sleeping Beauties at the Met

7 May 2024

by LUCY COATS

You glide up the steps in pretty
princess gowns, eyes blind, ears

deaf, parading what you call charity
before the cameras. In another place,

on this same night, bombs fall on tents,
screams rising like fireflies among

the smoke and ash, souls ripped
from starved bodies as easily

as butterfly wings, torn by cruel boys.
You are too busy sipping champagne

with gossip-rattle lips smeared with
fashionista killer red to notice the

tank crushing a brave sign that says
'I 🖤 Gaza' in defiance of all evidence
to the contrary. Nobody in or out now.
Everybody trapped like dying flies.

Murderers want no witnesses, but news arrives
anyway, on screens too used to dismissing horror.

And still you drink and drink and laugh, pretending
your filthy dollar gifts will make you somehow good.

Pompeii and Taxes

by HOLLIE ANDERSON

As Pompeii burns,
the coin is still counted.
Taxes are collected,
ash falls, and life is measured in bills.

Greed chases humanity as a dog does its tail.
Jormungandr feeds silently—
an eternal feast of self-consumption.

Whether in Rome or on Wall Street,
the flames will dance,
so long as the ledger is full.

But when the feast turns,
the rich will be devoured—
by empty mouths with stomachs full of smoke,
torn apart by hollow hands,
ravenous for what they hoarded,
until nothing is left but the bones
of a forgotten empire.

Without Compassion a Eulogy is Just Reimbursement

by SANDER LABRUYÈRE

I roam the city: mothish men drunk on red light,
so terribly ugly in the dim, silvered neon.
How everything around me is a construct—
how everything around me implies
transaction of currency.
As the city is drunk on its own splendour,
electricity fires from lantern to lantern
(as does a bullet from a gun to the chest
of a man far away),
and a million orange T-shirts,
hats and flags flare up,
and I too get drunk *(hiep hiep hoera!)*, drunk
on what has remained like a fact for centuries,
nothing added but metal and contracts.
Marnixstraat, Frederik Hendrikstraat—
all of the streets here are named after
statesmen of the 16th century,
most of them remembered for their coin, despite
how it was never laid on the eyes of the dead.
I am not against such remembering,
I just mean to point out: without compassion,
a eulogy is just reimbursement.
How can I call this magnificent maple here in
Vondelpark a miracle when its soil
is the trampled spine-rubble of other peoples?
I do not mean atonement. I just mean to ask:
how much history is enough history
before we may cease repetition?

The Grocery Shopping Cult

by ANNE FEY

The supermarket is a temple
Here we offer money to the god of quantity
Here we offer time to the god of choice
Give us our daily discount
And deliver us from dissatisfaction
For you have the competitive prices
And the customer-friendliness
From seven until eleven.

The supermarket is the promised land
Catering to every appetite
Anticipating every craving
Obliviating our needs.

My cart remains empty
I stand out as an infidel
Unslaked by the aisles upon aisles of assortment.

There are no cans of compassion,
Crates of health, jars of freedom,
Bags of safety, boxes of joy,
Or bottles of love on the shelves.

The Human Cost

by UN LEE STEELE

Has Greed reached its peak?
Bleak House whispers—
Not yet!
Hollowed souls scour the streets,
labour to the edge of madness.
London: class-ridden,
bustling, the world's envy.

Justice slouches, yawning—
inheritances drained,
futures devoured.
Wealth feasts,
unburdened by mercy.
The streets, then and now,
no different for those who
toil too long.

Ever accelerating,
Money and might—
the twin gods flex
muscle the market.

Ticker tapes flicker—
Greed's relics.
A casino of algorithms,
fast, blind,
profits wrapped in the illusion.

Laws bend, loopholes
widen,
and ledger lines stretch
with unseen hands.

CAPITALISM IS A DEATH CULT

What a gig—
raking in a "mere" $4
billion a day?
No end in sight.
Still not satisfied

Gordon Gekko grins,
"Greed is good. Greed is never full."

For three decades now,
I've watched
the winners hoard
 boundless,
while the labourers sweat
blood
for wages
fixed to the clock
that moves too slowly.

The losers lose all,
digging their graves
with calloused hands,
watching justice slip
like crumbs between their fingers.
$7.25 an hour—
a decade past.
$8.25 today—
still a whisper,
barely enough for breath.

Untrained,
undereducated,
overeducated—
always unseen,
always unheard.

Greed wears many masks.

Sunday Mornings at the River

In the faceless crowd, it
feeds.
One voice rises—then vanishes.

Cry, if you will, for Maria Fernandes, 32—
kind, generous, lost in a foreign land.

Fluent in four languages,
a suitcase in her nineteen--
year-old hand.
Across the Atlantic, she flew,
Cinderella's dream
pressed to her brow.

America— Land of Opportunity—
offered no solace.

Three four shifts without end,
until sleep took her
forever, in the front seat of her car.
May her God receive her soul.

Greed has not yet met its summit—
Nine million die of
hunger each year worldwide.

Yet the billionaire ranks
swell, wealth rising faster than tides.

But can loss sustain greed's climb?

Unless we break free
from the progress,
built on the human cost.

If we do not act,
we will pay—
in hunger, in silence, in dust.

Seed-spitters
by ALEKSANDER ALEKSANDER

They sliced watermelons
and fed their bodies to summer children,
taught them to spit out black
seeds.

Indigestible, they said
afraid that those seeds would
grow
into sovereignty
of body and soil

They would rather starve
their children
of proteins and minerals
than see anyone free.

What a relief, they said
when seedless watermelons
filled fluorescent-lit aisles.

But the seed-spitters
splattered saliva-slick
black seeds

into vacant fenced lots,
between sidewalk cracks,
in alleys, in dumps,
oligarchal lawns

The seed-spitters
grew an autonomous garden.

Liberation is just spitting distance away.

When the Insomniacs

by HELEN VICTORIA MURRAY

we don't sleep anymore
we just lie here and wait

bask in the blue light naming
parts in which no rest is found

secular vespers are our sex now
begging the nothing to let us in

friends are tiring of their lovers
smiles chew through the inner cheek

leavings, the luxury
of overspend

we keep this house lit
with the doors locked

where once there was a velvet dark
moths are eating through the surface of our eyes

and we don't sleep anymore
we just lie

Uncomfortable Dichotomies

by ABBY BLAND

We live in a world where
you can buy a gold-embossed copy
of the Egyptian Book of the Dead
at Five & Below.
Nestled between
colouring books and decluttering guides
you'll find ancient spells
to shepherd the dead
through the underworld.

In this same world,
you can use WikiHow to
learn how to cleanse your crystals—
that you bought in bulk on Amazon—
using the selenite bowl
you bought on sale via Etsy.

After that, you can consult
the Google AI oracle
to find the 5 best methods
to cleanse your energy;
8 ways to charge your amethyst
in moonlight;
and 11 steps to cleansing
your Citrine with sage.

While this same world
we've stripped for parts
burns, and glaciers crash into
seas stretching their roaring waters
further and further
up on the quaking shores,
and the skies cry out in hurricanes.

I Don't Actually Want the Products, I Want to Look Like the Women Selling Me the Products

by MICHELLE AWAD

In this poem, I will prove that self-loathing is a multi-billion-dollar industry.

In the last two weeks, I have concluded
that I need to start contouring my face. It is too round in
all the wrong places. Every video I pause scrolling to view
features women I'm convinced are shapeshifters, their
bone structure changing like magic while I only look
good facing the sunlight coming in through a screen door
at midday. Only at one distinct angle. There is always a
money shot. And I know, because packages pile up at my
front door. Creams that will make my hair just wavy
enough to look like I did nothing to it, dresses to
camouflage my body into something worthy of want.

I am not buying stuff, I am buying aspirations, I am
buying possibilities, I am buying confidence too close to
its expiration date. If there is a shade of red lipstick I do
not own, it's because they haven't invented it yet. I have a
clear favourite, but some part of my brain is certain that
the next one will make me more desirable than I have
ever been. Every piece of shapewear chokes my hips, cuts
into my bikini line, strangles me like a punishment, the
cost of being smooth. Am I still the hottest girl in the
room if I'm irritable out of sheer discomfort? Are my lips
still kissable if they form a permanent grimace?

When I say I have an online shopping addiction, know
that I am lying.

When you say I have an online shopping addiction, know that is not accurate.

I don't have an addiction to online shopping. I have an addiction to unattainable beauty. I have an addiction to masking my insecurities. I have an addiction to comparing myself to other women when it is to my own detriment.

I imagine one day, I will shop myself thin. I will compress myself into oblivion.

I imagine one day, I will stop caring, but that's probably just another delusion.

Everyone I Went to High School With Is a Realtor Now

by MICHELLE AWAD

Meanwhile, on an unscreened back porch in Algiers, I'm sitting pondering whether I should start a Wiki Feet account. That's not to say I don't have a good job that pays well, but sometimes it's just nice to be wanted in a way you don't understand and can't explain.

Every now and then, I get this overwhelming sense of gaping, like a sinkhole forming in my centre, like my body is a thing that needs to be filled because it feels good to be whole after long periods of hollowed-outness.

Maybe you never outgrow the toxicity you were taught to love with, the bright red brushstrokes across a canvas that begs to be anything but white. Maybe I'm a fool for all this want.

So when I mention that everyone I went to high school with is a realtor now, what I mean is I wonder if anyone is really happy, if anyone is fulfilled in any meaningful way, or if the houses they sell are just a metaphor for emptiness. I wonder if this is what we all bargained for when we envisioned adulthood. I wonder if their souls are being fed and nurtured. I wonder if they're being touched like their thighs are the only water in a desert of lonely.

And when I mention that everyone I went to high school with is a realtor now, what I mean is I'm still a poet, same as I was when I was fifteen—only worse because now I post everything I write on the internet. I mean I'm still a girl who holds passion in higher esteem than comfort, intensity above sanity, and who can't seem to settle for anything else.

Corrupt...

by DONNA MCCABE

Tree of life—corrupted.
Money, power, and greed:
The fruits now bared,
Roots of all evil.

Solidarity

by FÉIDHLIM GLEESON

I had a panic attack this morning,
waking up from a shit shift
where my self-esteem was sliced,
diced and served alive
straight off the restaurant's marble counter,
one hundred and forty-five crowns an hour.

Sucking persimmons from Spain,
like a seventeenth-century king,
I watch the little yellow-breasted birds
peck moss from my tree,
jerking their heads
like tiny robots scanning for life,
terrifying tinier things.

Should they be here? It's snowing.
Are the streetlights blinding their great escape,
like a hungry child
forced to look a flashlight in the eye?
Is my tree having a panic attack this morning?
Shaking scaly hungry bird-feet
off its should-be sleeping back?

We resonate at the same frequency,
the dial turned up too high.
Next shift, I try to save as many scraps
of paper napkin
in my pocket as I can.
I continue to be sliced.

Neither True nor False: Found Poem from Job Application Screenings

by MEGAN FOLEY

I am patient at work / I am always prepared / I am sociable and outgoing / Others respect me/
I work hard / I pay my bills on time / My chores get done right away / I try to do my best /
I feel like I am a successful person / I can handle stress or pressure / I believe that life is a big game to be played with / I've "got my act together" / I have lots of energy / I get up easily in the morning / I like this period in my life / I am satisfied with who I am / I do not hurt people I love / I do not feel guilty/ I like to work

I am lonely / I get stressed out easily / I do things to attract attention / I worry about things/ Throughout my life I have not kept up with my peers socially / I am easily discouraged / I find life boring / I like to get lost in thought / I change my mood a lot / I believe in the importance of art / I often feel discouraged / I panic easily / I am afraid of being rejected / My moods change / I get blamed for things I didn't do / I am able to manipulate others / I am easily manipulated by others / I wonder what people are thinking of me / I am uncertain of my worth / I feel like I'm "just going through the motions" / I am lazy / I worry about what I am going to do with the rest of my life / I am full of ideas

We Aren't Ready to Pay the Full Price

by ARINA TROSTYANETSKAYA

The whiteness of winter only one day in
November out the window on a lunch break,
only early morning's frost biting the green grass,
only on friends' stories from further north.

Here we wear the same puffy jackets
bought on spring sales,
crochet hats and knitted Sophie's
scarves we made for each other as gifts,
converting inflation-to-income ratio
into expressions of self, or care.

It's sales cats-and-dogs, the whirlwind of prices
falling everywhere-all-around is meant to take
your breath away and delay you on your way home,
just like a snowstorm would
when you were a child.

At thirty-eight you find yourself disenchanted
from brightly-lit promises of beauty
and perfection at your fingertips.

To think how easy it used to be —Infatuated—
half an ear chopped off, caked blood
on a weird hat. I crochet for no one
else but myself, and a tear
the size of a knob.

There will be a dawn after a long dusk of
disillusionment, I'm just not there yet
to report back.

My mother gets tense when I mention my
therapist; my therapist gets tense
when I mention my mother, so I had to quit,
even though I was ready to keep paying if
only to allow myself to sit down.

But since then I had a dream with an unfamiliar
grey cat in it, half its ear chopped clean off,
caked blood in its fur, a tear in its eye
the size of a knob.

I started looking for sharp edges under closets,
bookcases, between kitchen cabinets, hoping
to find the place where the cat could have
ripped its ear off so cleanly.

Does anybody know if therapists have
Christmas offers?

Cruel Optimism

by JJ CAREY

"A relation of cruel optimism exists when something you desire is actually an obstacle to your flourishing." - Lauren Berlant

My boss defends the rich as if one day he'll be one of them. Nirvana will be a department store with no maths at the till. He will peacock with his sweet plump belly, his teetering crown

and its hushed arrow fireworks. Paradise will be the next car up in the range. The extension with a sky light. Herringbone parquet.
He'll have the best nativity on the street & a fresh drive each May.

Let's say there's some kind of boat. The hole in water where he throws his notes. His charming wasting asset, lilting giddy on the dock dance, all golden hope and empty banquette. You know the ropes, the rig.

Is it promise enough to trade for eternal 8am?
An endless reel of *not-yet not-yet not-today?* We're the mice, fighting over cheese high up in the eaves on Philpot Lane. Ready to eat. Just to drop.

That constant itch in the centre of your back will not be reached alone. The solstice comes when the sun stands still. Spilling glitter on pristine sea. The wake is turbulence. It follows the vessel like starving petrels.

The Wood-Runner's Sons

by ELIZABETH DEAN

Dear Hudson's Bay Company,
How does it taste?
Eradication.
Owing to a human god
Green and greed-ridden
Titanic
to your eighty stores.

You
do not have enough
of you
in you
to match
coin for coin
cent for cent
hair for hair
The ikwewag
Ininiwag
Women
Men
Children
More
Your traders made quad-striped
Smallpox blankets
for.

Dear Hudson's Bay Company,
How does it feel?
Evaporation.
What does it mean to be a dollar
Instead of a man?

Sunday Mornings at the River

Men have graves.

You
fade.
Hands waved
Street paved
Plaques unlaid
Billion paid.

Without trace
Erased.

Dear Hudson's Bay Company,

They outlived you.

You are not people.

People survive.

People endure.

People

wait.

There Is No Money

by ELIZABETH DEAN

I reach into my pockets,
Scout the worn-down grey-thread seams
Of my jeans
It seems
My trailing fingertips
Without a cent conclude
There is no money.

I reach for my wallet
Find credit and debit
Bus pass falls onto the floor
And I let it
With bills go thrills
And life in the Hills
These plastic friends from the bank are useless
And I begrudgingly accept it
There is no money.

Did you know zinc and copper evaporate
Gold-tinged polar bear toonies don't conglomerate
Inside the piggy banks of the people who need it
Who smash them open
To bits and shatter-shards
Life is hard
These people who swallow lives full of zeroes before the decimal
Know all too well that
There is no money.

While I stride through the bus stops of Toronto downtown
All the companies sing but no one is around
Not a soul, not a hope, not a dime to be found

Only backhoes and cranes digging up the fresh ground
And I wonder for whom and for exactly what crowd
Do they build up these condos
Charge us double, pound for pound
Don't they know that
There is no money.

As the numbers descend
Bank balance comes to an end
I see the tumbling digits
Reflect in the eyes of my friend
And her neighbour
And her sister
That random stranger
And mister
They didn't bury their gold in the ground
Why can't it be found
Why is it that
There is no money.

They put Galen Weston on the stand
As if that would tie his hands
And liberate lettuce
And milk dumped despite the demand
While patients' vitals crashed
Profit records were smashed
And when asked how, they said
People spent more
And the interest rate soared
We are poor
If you weighed this city in gold
You would mourn
As I mourn
That this poem was ever born
And would find that
There is no money.

CAPITALISM IS A DEATH CULT

The stock market it rose
Common man's assets froze
We are worth less
As rich man's worth more
On Bali beaches sunny
Perhaps finding it funny
Our heatless complaints
They must bore
Such a chore
To feel sorry and sore
For the peasantry poor
And their suffering in store.

Remember, you remember
Remember, remember
The sun-drenched man
Pocketing wallets and land
And his kin
And his sin

They are why
There is no money.

Slaves to Capitalism

by MWELWA CHILEKWA

Interwoven into our DNA is the impulse to submit
stitched into our strands is suppression
dread, tax-free, is passed down generations
at birth, doctors cut the cord but they close their eyes
to the chain around our ankles
cross-legged we cower on the assembly line,
programmed with propaganda
they name our protection, Capitalism
born to bow before our saviour

As children we are read fairy tales and applaud
when the prince slips on Cinderella's shoe
we extensively study hundreds of years of history
blissfully unaware of how they bleach it
told stories of those who make it to the top
with their hands hidden to conceal the blood
they call themselves our role models — we can be rich too!

We grow to become adults,
excited for what was promised us
but when opportunity knocks,
the door is fastened with a silver spoon
entrepreneurship is sailing, the majority left lost at sea
drowning in cover letters and CVs,
barely able to afford a degree or a suit for an interview
while the government spends taxes on more anti-homeless architecture

CAPITALISM IS A DEATH CULT

People are still dying and when we ask why,
the finger is pointed in our direction —
we are not working enough, we are not earning enough,
we are not enough
even the ballot is another gaslight
one more one-percenter with the same story
but we are too old for fairytales now

Our ancestors fought for freedom,
yet we have a new slave master
who rigs the deck then deals our cards
placing us on a scale for inspection
evaluates what class we are
by our background, ethnicity, ability
ignoring all humanity
stamping a price tag on our foreheads
ready to sell to the highest bidder. No longer.

We may be born to bow but
we are also born to bleed for what we believe in.
See you at the rebellion.

About the Contributors

Abby Bland (she/they) is a spoken word artist and poet whose solo show Godzilla's Not A Dinosaur won "Best of Venue" at the 2023 KC Fringe. A two-time Best Spoken Word Artist winner in The Pitch, Abby's work appears widely. Follow on Instagram @applestoabby or visit abbyblandpoetry.com.

Afon Gold is confused; but that's the one word trans people must never use because society uses this as evidence that they are a phase, a fallacy, or a product of folly. They write and persist in the space between the natural world and one of commerce/greed.

Aleksander Aleksander is seven magpies in a trench coat and an emerging writer documenting empire collapse. Their work appears in Gnashing Teeth Press, Citizen Trans {Project}, Ambrosia Zine, and others. They drift between the Salish Sea and Great Plains and can be found at aleksanderaleksander.com and in their newsletter, seedgiver.

Allen Ashley is a British Fantasy Award-winning writer, poet and editor based in London. His latest chapbook, Journey to the Centre of the Onion (Eibonvale Press, 2023), blends speculative and slipstream themes. His work has appeared in The World of Myth, Sein und Werden, Focus, and BFS Horizons. He also leads Clockhouse London Writers, an advanced SFF writing group.

Arina Trostyanetskaya is a poet, dancer, and founder of Poetry Unleashed in Copenhagen. She writes with her body's memory, shaped by years of contemporary dance. Her work appears in NU magazine (Super Books, 2025). @arinamoves and @poetry_unleashed_cph.

b.c. pellegrini (they/them) is a queer, trans poet and anticapitalist from Italy. Their work appears in Songs of

Revolution, 2025 Poetry Diary, We Are All Palestinians, and more. You can find them on Instagram @bc.pelle.

Charlotte Renner is a writer based in New York. She has lived in many places, and considers them all home. You can find her on Instagram @mildscorpio.

Claire Kroening is a poet and prose writer based in the upper Midwest. Their work has been published in New Words Press, Young Writers Journal, Indie Earth Publishing, and more. When not writing, they can be found exploring coastlines. Find them on Instagram @clairerosek.

Donna McCabe is a poet from South Wales, UK, with over twenty years of publication history. Her work appears in journals and anthologies worldwide. She shares poetry via Instagram @donnamccabe_ and on Facebook at Poems by Donna McCabe.

Edward Alport is a retired teacher and former international business executive and City slicker. Currently a poet, writer and gardener. He has had poetry, articles and stories published various webzines and magazines and performed on BBC Radio and Edinburgh Fringe. . His Bluesky handle is @crossmouse.bsky.social. His website is crossmouse.wordpress.com

Elizabeth Dean (she/they) is a multidisciplinary artist and storyteller from Mississauga, Ontario. Her work is anti-capitalist, anti-colony, and pro-community. She hosts the podcast Retrospect Station and performs spoken word across Canada. @astroalex34

Ellen Harrold is an Irish artist, writer, and editor-in-chief of Metachrosis Literary. Her work explores anatomy and physics through abstraction. She publishes in both English and Irish and exhibits across Ireland and the UK. @ellenharroldart

Féidhlim Gleeson (he/they) is an Irish poet and performer living in Copenhagen. They write as a form of rest. Their work appears in Sunday Mornings at the River and upcoming Copenhagen anthologies. Their bicycle is named Eugene.

Flavian Mark Lupinetti is a Pushcart-nominated poet, fiction writer, and cardiac surgeon. When he wrote this poem in 2022, he was told it was "over the top." He took it as a compliment. His debut collection, The Pronunciation Part, was published by The Poetry Box in 2025.

Frederick Pollack is the author of six poetry collections, including The Adventure, Happiness, and The Liberator. His work has appeared widely in print and online journals. He lives and writes in Washington, DC. www.frederickpollack.com

Giorgia Cipolloni —also known as Gia—is a writer, photographer, and student from Rome, now based in Copenhagen. She lives with her typewriter, her cameras, and a creative kind of chaos. More at gior-gia.com.

Helen Victoria Murray is a Glaswegian writer and researcher. Her work explores weird houses, obsolete formats, and bodies with shifting boundaries. She publishes across fiction, poetry, and criticism. More at helenvictoriamurray.com / @helenvmurray

J.J. Carey is a queer Irish poet based in Leeds. A finalist for the Tempest and Oxford Poetry Prizes in 2024, their work appears in Beyond the Veil, Mobius, and more. More at jjcarey.com.

Jillian Adel is a multidisciplinary artist and poet based in Los Angeles. Her work explores the mystical, personal, and philosophical. She runs Studio of Earthly Delights and the esoteric practice Vague Intellectual Pleasure. @JillianBAdel

John O'Hare is a Bristol-based writer and artist exploring mental health and masculinity through poetry and visual work. His writing has appeared in The Manchester Review, Fleas on the Dog, The Poetry Lighthouse, and Sunday Mornings at the River. Website: www.johnohare.org.uk.

Jordon Briggs is a creative and thinker living in Oakland,CA. His work explores nuanced human experiences, media, culture, and history. More at jordonbriggs.com and @briggs_jordon_

Joseph Nutman is a poet from North Hertfordshire. His work has been published by Sunday Mornings at the River, Shearsman, Acid Bath Publishing, Cambridge Poetry, and Spelt. He was shortlisted for the 2024 Cheltenham International Poetry Festival Competition.

Kali Joy Cramer (he/she) is from the Chicago suburbs. A recipient of the 2024 Ireland Chair of Poetry Student Award, his work has appeared in Impossible Archetype, Relief, and The Broken Spine.

Kate Gough is a poet based in the Treaty 7 region of Canada. Her work blends romantic sensibilities with themes of trauma and chronic illness. She has three books with Sunday Mornings at the River. @chamomilde on Instagram and YouTube.

Kate MacAlister is a poet, filmmaker, and feminist organiser. She's published globally, runs multilingual arts projects, and leads poetry workshops for women and genderqueer creatives. Her latest collections are out with Querencia Press and Sunday Mornings at the River. @kissed.by_fire

Kate Smith (she/her) is a poet and journalist based in Washington. Her work explores mental health, queerness, and nature. She appears in Dear Survivor and We Do Not Need Permission to Rise (Beyond the Veil Press).

Leah Keane is an Irish poet living in Freiburg, Germany. Her work has appeared in Poetry Ireland Review, Skylight 47, ROPES and more. She's currently working on her first collection. @l.keane113

Lee Sheridan is an Irish poet, songwriter, and novelist. He runs Luain Press and has published St George's Day and Monuments. His work has appeared in Drawn to the Light Press and several competitions across Ireland.

Lewis Wyn Davies is a Shropshire-based poet whose work appears in Poetry Wales, The Pomegranate London, and Dreich. He's read live at Westminster Music Library, BBC Radio, and iamb. @poemsbylewis

Lucy Coats is a neurodivergent poet based in Northamptonshire, UK. Her work weaves together nature, feminism, grief, Celtic folklore, and queerness. She is currently working on her debut collection and a book about matriarchal goddesses. @lucywriter on Instagram and Threads.

Malavika Suresh is a writer, performer, and researcher from Dubai. Her work explores selfhood and society, and has been featured across the UAE and internationally. She merges sociology and poetry at @malspeaks_.

Mateo X is a writer, editor, and musician based in the DC area. His work explores power, place, and the search for connection. His debut EP The Greed is streaming now. Find him @iammateox on Instagram.

Megan Foley is a queer poet and artist who writes sad poems and makes unhinged art. Her manuscript Survival Exhibits was longlisted for the Dzanc Poetry Prize. She holds an MFA from Regis University.

Michael Brigden writes as The Ordinary Poet. His poetry—often inspired by love, frustration, and awe—appears across global anthologies and on social media. A romantic at heart, Michael draws from the world around him and the life he shares with his family.

Nathaniel Krenkel is a writer and music producer based in Portland, Maine. He hosts Rhizome Radio at WMPG and runs the record labels Team Love and Oystertones. His writing lives at the intersection of sound, memory, and place. nathanielkrenkel.com

Paul atten Ash is the pen name of Bristol-based writer, composer, and art-photographer Paul Nash. His poetry has appeared in Magma, Under the Radar, Poetry Scotland, and on BBC Radio 6 Music. His debut pamphlet Searchlight Seasons was published in 2024. He has been shortlisted for the Ginkgo, Alpine Fellowship, and Hexham poetry prizes.

Rachel Berryman is a sustainable energy technologist and poet living in Berlin. Her writing explores the moral weight of technological progress. Her poems have appeared in OPEN, Beyond Words, and others. She publishes essays via her Substack, Unfurl Poetry.

Raidah Kazi is a writer and student from Dhaka, Bangladesh. She splits her time between university, writing for The Daily Star, and crafting her own work—poetry, prose, or something in between. She believes in spaces that welcome the unpolished and unafraid.

Rajani Radhakrishnan lives in Bangalore, India. She has published two poetry collections and has been nominated for the Pushcart Prize and Best of the Net. Her work often explores memory, identity, and language.

Rebecca Rijsdijk is a writer, carer, and lifelong dissident raised in the woods of the Netherlands. She believes poetry should unsettle, awaken, and unearth what the system would rather keep buried. When she's not fighting burnout or empire, she runs her own poetry press, Sunday Mornings at the River. rebeccarijsdijk.com

Robert Frede Kenter is a poet, hybrid writer, visual artist, and publisher of Ice Floe Press. His work has appeared internationally and he has received Pushcart and Best of the Net nominations. His latest book, Father Tectonic, was published by Ethel Press in 2025. He lives online at @icefloe22 and r.f.k.vispocityshuffle.

Rose Winter (she/her) is a Belfast-based writer of poetry, fiction, and the strange spaces between. Her work appears in The Honest Ulsterman, The Apiary Magazine, and Unlatched Podcast. @rosewinter.00

R. Gerry Fabian is a poet and writer from Doylestown, Pennsylvania. He has published five poetry collections, including Pilfered Circadian Rhythm and Ball on the Mound, a poetry book about baseball. His work is known for its clarity, rhythm, and quiet power.

Ruth Lexton is an English teacher and poet whose work has appeared in Abridged, Shooter, Ink, Sweat & Tears, and The Alchemy Spoon. She won second prize in the 2023 Hexham Poetry Competition and was longlisted for the 2023 Aurora Prize.

Sam Huang is a nonbinary lesbian Asian American writer and student. Their poetry has been published in fifth wheel press, engendered*, and Healthline Zine. They also write for FilmCred and host two Substacks: everything matters to me and every song I've ever loved.

Samuel Forbes writes from the foothills of Pikes Peak. A poet of quiet resilience, he writes to keep the small flame in his soul burning bright.

Sarah Beck Mather is an artist, actress, and poet published in Sunday Mornings at the River, Bloodmoon Poetry Mag, and Streetcake Magazine. She creates visual poetry and performs across literary and arts magazines.

Sarah Blakely is a California-based poet whose work explores sexual violence, healing, and women's rights. Her poems have appeared in various anthologies and the 2024 issue of Timberline Review. She was shortlisted for the 2025 Central Avenue Poetry Prize. You can find her work on Instagram @sarahb.poetry.

Sarah Gawthrop writes from the unceded territories of the Semiahmoo First Nation in so-called Canada. She is a poet, editor, and BFA creative writing major and sits on The Wee Sparrow Poetry Press, pulp and ROOM Magazine boards. Sarah's work has appeared in print publications by pulp MAG, Gypsophila Magazine, and Humana Obscura, among others. Connect with her on social media @sarahjeanninewrites

Sharjeel H Tiwana is a bilingual poet, essayist, and multidisciplinary artist based in Rawalpindi, Pakistan. His work explores the personal and the political, and has appeared in Youth Dissent, Pen and Paper Mag, and Gypsophila Magazine. He has performed at Cassette Kahani and uses his creative work to support progressive causes in his community. @sharjeel.h.tiwana

Sonya Soni (she/her) is a Brooklyn-based poet, prison abolitionist, and the descendant of Punjabi freedom fighters. She designs poetry workshops for systems-impacted youth and writes about diasporic dreaming and radical solidarity. @sonyasoni8

Soph Kay is a queer poet, knowledge enthusiast and AuDHDer. Their work can be found in various places under various names including the Transmotion journal and other works from Sunday Mornings at the River. When they're not writing they're co-directing the New Voices in Postcolonial Studies Network.

Tomás Laorni Manopulo is a non-binary Italian-Colombian artist who expresses their love through food and poetry. For Tomás, nourishment is art, and community is resistance. Their work is rooted in connection, care, and slow revolutions.

Uzomah Ugwu is a poet, curator, and multidisciplinary artist whose work centres on human rights, mental health, and LGBTQIA+ justice. She is the author of The Triumph of Sorrow: A Lover of Longing and the founder and managing editor of Arte Realizzata.

Vikki C. is a British-born writer with work in over 80 international venues. She has been nominated for the Pushcart Prize, Best of the Net, and the Orison Best Spiritual Literature. Her latest collection Where Sands Run Finest was published by DarkWinter Press in 2024. Instagram: @vikkic.author

About the Publisher

Sunday Mornings at the River is a poetry publisher that is dedicated to elevating and amplifying the voices of poets who are often marginalized or overlooked by the traditional publishing world.

At Sunday Mornings at the River, we are committed to creating a thriving literary community that is based on healthy and inclusive collaborations. We believe that everyone has the right to be heard, and we strive to provide a platform for poets to share their work with a wider audience.

Our focus is on publishing poetry that is thought-provoking, challenging, and that speaks to the unnameable aspects of the human experience. We believe that poets have the power to name the frauds, take sides, start arguments, and shape the world, and we are always on the lookout for new voices that are pushing the boundaries of traditional poetry.

As an independent publisher, we are dedicated to promoting equality and inclusivity in all our endeavours. Whether we are working with established authors or helping emerging poets to get their work out into the world, we are committed to creating a welcoming and supportive environment for poets of all backgrounds and experiences.

Scan me
for more books
by Sunday Mornings
at the River

w: sundaymorningsattheriver.com
e: hello@sundaymorningsattheriver.com
ig: @sundaymorningsattheriver

www.ingramcontent.com/pod-product-compliance
Lightning Source LLC
LaVergne TN
LVHW041950070526
838199LV00051BA/2966